More Praise for Brian L. Patton and *The Sexy Vegan Cookbook*

"One of the most important actions we can take to protect the environment is adopting a plant-based diet, and *The Sexy Vegan Cookbook* makes that task easier than ever. Armed with creative faux meats and a lighthearted approach, Brian Patton takes the daunting endeavor of eating healthily, ethically, and environmentally consciously and makes it an easy (and incredibly delicious) pill to swallow. Reserve a spot on your bookshelf for this one. It's a must-have!"

— Ed Begley, Jr., actor, activist, and author of *Living Like Ed: A Guide to the Eco-Friendly Life*

"In these pages, chef Brian Patton shows you that veganism can be sexy and delicious."

— Rod Rotondi, author of *Raw Food for Real People*

"In his videos, Brian Patton has a unique blend of talents, genuine charisma, and an ardent streak of irreverence that is most refreshing. [He is] very successful in making veganism look practical and accessible instead of 'fluffy' or esoteric. Stick with it! I can feel Alton Brown shaking in his calfskin wingtips."

— Chris D., a viewer in the Midwest

THE SEXY VEGAN COOKBOOK

THE SEXY VEGAN COOKBOOK

EXTRAORDINARY FOOD from an Ordinary Dude

BRIAN L. PATTON

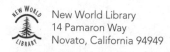

New World Library
14 Pamaron Way
Novato, California 94949

The Sexy Vegan™ and The Sexy Vegan logo are registered trademarks of Brian L. Patton.
Photo credits: Dan Boissy: 161; Hilary McHone: viii, 10, 22, 40–41, 60–61, 78, 91, 100, 106, 110, 113, 120, 156, 174
Text design by Tracy Cunningham
Typography by Tracy Cunningham and Tona Pearce Myers

Library of Congress Cataloging-in-Publication Data
Patton, Brian L., date.
The sexy vegan cookbook : extraordinary food from an ordinary dude / Brian L. Patton.
    p.   cm.
Includes index. · 4822 9818 ⁷/₁₂
ISBN 978-1-60868-045-0 (pbk. : alk. paper)
1. Vegan cooking. 2. Cookbooks. I. Title.
TX837.P339 2012
641.5'636—dc23

2011048788

First printing, March 2012
ISBN 978-1-60868-045-0
Printed in Canada on 100% postconsumer-waste recycled paper

New World Library is proud to be a Gold Certified Environmentally Responsible Publisher.
Publisher certification awarded by Green Press Initiative. www.greenpressinitiative.org

10 9 8 7 6 5 4 3 2 1

"Live long and prosper."

— MR. SPOCK,

science officer, first officer,

commanding officer,

federation ambassador,

vegan

Contents |||||||||||||||||||||||||||||||||||||||||||||||||||||||||||||||||||||||||||||||||||||||||||||||||||||||||||||||

CHAPTER 1.
THE MOST IMPORTANT MEAL OF THE DAY... Cocktails!

CHAPTER 2.
BEATIN' THE MEAT   Meat Substitutes

CHAPTER 3.
THE SECOND MOST IMPORTANT MEAL OF THE DAY, AFTER COCKTAILS   Breakfast

CHAPTER 4.
SPOON-FED Soups

CHAPTER 5.
GO FORK YOURSELF! Salads

CHAPTER 6.
HANDHELD Sandwiches

CHAPTER 7.
THE DINNER BELL Entrees

CHAPTER 8.
PIZZA!!

CHAPTER 9.
SNACKAGE

CHAPTER 10.
CONDIMENTS AND SAUCES

BONUS CHAPTER.
WE ALL SCREAM!! Ice Cream

Acknowledgments ||||||||||||||||||||||||||||||||||||||||||||||||||||||||||||||

FIRST I'D LIKE TO THANK MY PARENTS, Lynn and Enrico Patton. They never laid any messed-up trips on me when I was a kid, and as a result I ended up fairly well-adjusted. They didn't bat an eye when I became vegan, and always showed interest in my new lifestyle. They also had the foresight to plant that money tree in the backyard. Good work, guys!

Second, I'd like to thank the Girlfriend. She was pretty much my only taste-tester during the production of this book and gave me very valuable feedback. So if any of these recipes suck, blame her. While she doesn't act like a chef (since chefs actually cook on occasion), she definitely thinks like one. That, along with the moral support and love she gave and continues to give, and a few XXX-rated activities slipped in for good measure, helped me get through the writing of this book. And while she never, of course, had to, she promised to tell me if any of my jokes or stories weren't funny or good. Thanks, babe!

Finally, I'd like to thank that ballsy crew over at New World Library. Cover designer extraordinaire Tracy Cunningham: thank you for being the creative dynamo behind the perfect cover and design. The great Ami Parkerson: thank you for showing my videos to the editor, thus plucking me out of obscurity and thrusting me into semi-obscurity. To expert publicist Kim Corbin: without you, this complete stranger would probably not be holding this book right now

— they wouldn't even be aware of its existence. Finally to Kristen Cashman, Jonathan Wichmann, and the whole editorial staff: thank you for taking my ramblings and molding them into relative coherence. You make me look good! Even more finally, a super special thanks to Georgia Hughes who carefully guided my newbie ass through this crazy process: thank you for everything — you are my Obi-Wan Kenobi of book writing.

Introduction ||||||||||||||||||||||||||||||||||||||||||||||||||||||||||||||||||||||||||||||

HELLO, PEOPLE! Sexy Vegan here...wait a second...*here*? Where is here? Where am I? Am I in a book? How the hell did this happen? Hmm...I guess we should rewind.

Once upon a time, in early May of 1977, my dad got into my mom's pants, thus planting a seed, which eventually sprouted arms, legs, and, thankfully, a head. Shortly after this seed was sown, with my tiny, gelatinous, cellular self forming in my mommy's belly, my parents went to see a new, state-of-the-art movie called *Star Wars*. I only mention this because it marked a turning point in my life: it thrust me into geekdom faster than the *Millennium Falcon* did the Kessel Run (which, incidentally, was less than twelve parsecs...very fast). About nine months after that, on February 16, 1978, in Hazleton, Pennsylvania, I was welcomed into the world by being carved out of my mother's womb, because I was all upside down and shit.

Then one day I went to college. Four years, two beer-pong trophies, countless blackouts, and one miraculous diploma later, I ended up on my parents' couch...for a year...which I *know* they loved. While enjoying this much-needed "time to chill," I happened upon a local-access cooking show. It was hosted by a portly, balding fellow with a mustache named Chef Lou (that was *his* name, not his mustache's). He made an angel-hair pasta dish, of diced tomatoes, garlic, butter, basil, and Parmesan, and presented it so simply that I didn't even need to write it down. Keep in mind, I had not learned how to cook spaghetti until my senior year of college. But watching Chef Lou, I thought, "I can do that," and the next day, I did it. I made it for dinner, my parents loved it, and I sensed that they were just a little less disappointed in me than usual.

Finally, in October 2001, I decided to strike out on my own and join the real world…so I moved to Hollywood, for no other reason than that one of my friends was moving there, and I had nothing better to do. So we loaded up the car and trucked across the country. After a few friendless, penniless, shitty job–having years, I found myself unemployed with zero direction. Tinseltown, my ass!

In those first few years, however, I did get addicted to cooking shows. I would TiVo episodes featuring dishes that I thought I could make, and then transfer them to VHS tape to keep "on file." My roommate said he didn't know what made me a bigger loser: that I was painstakingly preserving episodes of *30 Minute Meals* or that I was trying to conceal their existence by labeling them *Star Trek*. I didn't care, though — I was too concerned with how terrible of a cook I was, but I *did* enjoy the process.

I don't really know where that enjoyment came from. I grew up in an Italian family, but I had a mother who hated to cook. Sure, we would get the occasional pancake breakfast or some sort of Crock-Pot thing for dinner, but for the most part, we ate pizza. Pizza with sausage, pizza with pepperoni, cheesesteak pizza, and don't even get me started on the stromboli. There were some really great pizza joints in town, and we had them all on speed dial. There were simply no vegetables to speak of, and I don't even think I knowingly consumed a bean until I moved to California.

I do remember my grandmother and my great-grandmother — or Little Nana and Big Nana, as we called them — making huge Sunday dinners. After having a little Jesus wafer amuse-bouche at church, we rolled on down to the grandparents' house for the weekly feast. Homemade pasta, ravioli, meatballs, sausage, tomato sauce, and Italian bread, all from scratch. Their kitchen looked like a bomb had hit it, but the aromas and flavors were out of this world. I can't imagine what time Big and Little Nana had to get up in the morning to feed fifteen people by noon, but I do know that my other grandmother, on my mom's side of the family, goes to bed at 6 PM, wakes up at midnight, and starts cooking. Maybe this is where I get my enjoyment for cooking...and as I age, my sleep schedule seems to be moving in that direction as well.

Back to being a fat, jobless, twenty-six-year-old loser. Oh, I didn't mention *fat* before? Yeah, I'm about 5 feet 9 inches, and I was pushing 260 pounds at the time. As depressed and directionless as I was, I did see my unemployment as an opportunity to choose a path. My cooking got to the point that I felt just confident enough to serve my food to other humans, and since I had no interest in utilizing my $100,000 public relations degree (something else I know my parents really *loved*), I thought this would be a great time to see exactly how much I enjoyed preparing food, so I tried doing it for a living.

I found an online ad looking for a cook to work at a (now defunct) little cafe in Culver City called On Higher Grounds. It served breakfast, sandwiches, burgers, salads, and soups. I thought these were all things I could handle, so I called. I went in for the interview, and this is where I met the great chef Teri Gooden. She was running the kitchen for her friend who owned the joint. She must have seen something in me during our conversation, or perhaps she was responding to the fact that I offered to work for free, but she hired me on the spot, with zero professional experience.

On Higher Grounds was, for me, more or less a crash course in everything food. I don't mean just making the dishes; I mean prepping, prioritizing, organizing, taking inventory, produce ordering, shopping — essentially managing the entire operation of the kitchen. Chef Teri showed me the ropes, teaching me a great deal about not only food but also efficiency and organization. After a couple of months, she began devoting all her time to her catering company, In Good Taste L.A. (she gave me my start, so, yes, she gets a plug — she's awesome!), and left me to run the cafe. We were staffed with one waitress, one dishwasher, and myself, period. No assistant. No backup. Was it stressful? Yes. Did I want to drive my car off the Santa Monica Pier on a daily basis? Yes. Am I totally awesome for being able to effectively handle all this with no prior experience? Yes. It was also an experience of inestimable value, and I will forever thank Chef Teri for all she taught me…plus, she paid me for every single hour that I worked, which was nice.

Something, however, just didn't feel quite right. Despite the stresses, I enjoyed doing the job, but I was left feeling somewhat unfulfilled, and I wasn't sure why. I was feeding people food they wanted, it tasted good, and it was of good quality, but deep down I thought there was almost a frivolousness to it. Not specifically to the food I was preparing there, but to the more complex food that I imagined I would prepare in the future if I continued to more up-scale endeavors. I had the mentality more of a home cook than of a professional chef. I didn't want to be extravagant or wasteful. I wanted there to be more value in the food that I prepared than just tantalizing people's taste buds, but I didn't know what other value there could be. This led me to seriously question my career path. As I was writing this section I came across a quotation from Marianne Williamson that pretty much summed up my feelings at the time: "The most important question to ask about any work is: 'How does this serve the world?'"

Since I'm not on "Oprah's Favorite Things" mailing list (any-more), I didn't know who this Marianne Williamson was. But when one of my hippie Twitter friends tweeted her quote, I was so happy that someone had given me the perfect words to describe my plight at the time that I retweeted it immediately. (By the way, if you don't know what all this "tweeted," and "retweeted" stuff is about...congratulations! You have a life!)

Now, don't worry, we're getting to the part where I become a supersuccessful vegan cookbook author, but I have to become vegan first.

During my time at On Higher Grounds, I was also aware of Vegin' Out, a small weekly vegan delivery service that my friend Dan Boissy and his brother owned (where I am currently executive chef). They were running the business out of their apartment and wanted to expand into a commercial kitchen, so I worked it out that they could rent the kitchen at On Higher Grounds on Sunday nights, when we were closed. They also asked me to cook with them, and I said, "Sure!"

After about six months, they offered me a full-time position doing marketing during the week and prepping the food Sunday nights. I had been at On Higher Grounds for a year and a half, so I was definitely ready to move on. I gave them my two weeks' notice and became a full-time employee of Vegin' Out.

Being the only meat eater working for Vegin' Out, I thought I'd try becoming vegan for a month. Remember, I weighed in at a whopping 260 pounds, and I thought this little, one-month "diet" would give me a solid kick start to getting back into shape. Actually, "getting back into shape" implies that I was once in shape. To clarify, there had been only about forty-eight months of my life where I was actually in shape, and nine of those months I was in utero. So I was really just hoping to get *in* shape.

On September 10, 2006, I cooked myself up a nice porterhouse with mushroom gravy and some roasted potatoes, and the next day

I went vegan. I realize that this means my first day of being vegan was on September 11th, but I wasn't making any symbolic statement; it just happened to be a Monday, and, as we all know, diets start on Monday.

After this animal product–free month, I had more energy and I'd lost about eight pounds, so I thought I'd give it another month, and then another month. My energy continued to skyrocket, and my doodie became more and more, um…attractive, which was very nice. When you're an obese man, eating a terrible diet, your day kind of revolves around defecation. Your doodie schedule is unpredictable, and after you go, you don't really feel, um, right until you've showered. Wow, this really took a turn, huh? Everybody still hungry? Good. The point is, I was becoming healthy on the inside, which was beginning to show on the outside: my complexion improved, the whites of my eyes got whiter, and after ten months, I'd lost sixty pounds! The most important factor, however, is the doodie. It acts as a litmus test for your overall health…or should I say *shit-mus* test. Nice.

On the same level of importance as having consistently enjoyable bowel movements was the fact that my new way of life lent the value to my work that I had felt it was missing. I realized that consuming vegan food and preparing it for others served the world in countless positive ways. I certainly could have written about the health, ecological, and ethical benefits of a vegan diet, but that is a totally different book, for someone way, way smarter to write. The key is that once I discovered that I could not only survive but thrive without taking the life of another being, I was sold. I was a vegan. For good.

At some point, in late 2006, someone told me all about this YouTube.com website. I had not yet heard of it, but after they described it to me I said, "Wait, I can do *what*?!? And I can say bad words?" So I immediately began to ponder doing a silly online cooking show, for no other purpose than to entertain my friends and to distract me from a four-hour-a-day *Halo* habit. I shot it with the help of my trusty cameraman and longtime friend Crandall, and threw it up onto the interwebs. It was somehow featured on the how-to page on YouTube and jumped to 25,000 views in less than a month. So I continued to make episodes over the next couple of years, threw together a website and a MySpace page (RIP), and built up kind of a fan base, mostly in Canada for some reason (I love you guys!).

Then on January 15, 2010, pretty much out of nowhere I received an email from the great Georgia Hughes of New World Library, asking me if I would want to write a cookbook. I immediately thought, "Hmm…I don't even *read* books, but okay, I'll do that."

I, however, had to first do a little research on this Georgia character, simply to confirm that she was indeed a real person, from a real company, and not one of my idiot friends messing with me (which would not have been the first time). After concluding that Georgia was indeed real, I agreed to allow New World Library to pay me to write a book. So, here I am. In a book. It's papery in here. Enjoy!

WTF is this weird square thing?

It's a QR code. You'll find them sprinkled throughout the book, and they link to helpful videos of me demonstrating select recipes. To take advantage of this feature, simply download a QR code–reading app to your smartphone or tablet. I'll periodically update the links to offer bonus recipes and tips, so be sure to follow, like, and subscribe to the Sexy Vegan at my various social media outlets to keep yourself informed of the updates.

Scan to watch
the video.

www.thesexyvegan.com
www.facebook.com/thesexyvegan
www.twitter.com/thesexyvegan
www.youtube.com/lukin82

CHAPTER 1
The Most Important Meal
of the Day...
cocktails!

||||||||||||||||||||||||||||||||||||||||||||||||||||||||||||||||||||||||||||||||||||||||||||||||||||||||||||||||||

WHETHER YOU'RE GETTING TUNED UP before a night out, in need of a little "hair of the dog" the next morning, or having some civilized libations at a skinny jeans– and hoodie–clad hipster dinner party, these beverages are sure to positively affect both the palate and the blood alcohol content.

THE BLOODBATH

||||||||||||||||||||||||||||||||||||||||||||||||||||||||||||||||||||||||||||||||||||||||||||||||||||||||||||||||||||||||||||||||||||||||||||||||||||

I wouldn't call this one the "Breakfast of Champions" — it's more like the "Breakfast of Runners-Up." Adobo sauce is the delicious stuff in which canned chipotle peppers are packed. You can find it in the Mexican section of most markets.

Makes 1 cocktail

1 shot (1½ fluid ounces) vodka
1 cup canned, bottled, or fresh tomato juice
¼ teaspoon vegan Worcestershire sauce (see WTF below)
Pinch of salt
Pinch of pepper
Pinch of celery seed
¼ teaspoon adobo sauce
Celery stalk, for garnish

Fill a pint glass halfway with ice. In a cocktail shaker, combine the vodka, tomato juice, Worcestershire, salt, pepper, celery seed, and adobo. Shake for 5 seconds to mix thoroughly, and pour over the ice. Garnish with a celery stalk and any dignity or self-respect you may have dropped on the floor the night before.

WTF is not vegan about Worcestershire sauce?

Believe it or not, it's made with anchovies. There are, however, a few fantastic vegan versions out there. You can find vegan Worcestershire sauce at a natural foods market or on the interwebs.

THE ARNOLD BOMBER

The first three ingredients here make a killer lemonade. Just please be sure to always use fresh lemon juice in *all* your food preparation...or else you will be destroyed.

Makes 2 cocktails

½ cup fresh lemon juice
3 cups water
½ cup agave nectar
1 shot (1½ fluid ounces) rum
1 shot (1½ fluid ounces) vodka
1 shot (1½ fluid ounces) white tequila
1 shot (1½ fluid ounces) gin
½ shot (¾ fluid ounce) triple sec
8 ounces cola

In a pitcher or bowl, whisk together the lemon juice, water, and agave, and set aside. Fill a cocktail shaker halfway with ice, and add the rum, vodka, tequila, gin, and triple sec. Shake for 5 seconds to mix thoroughly. Fill two pint glasses halfway with ice cubes and strain the contents of the shaker into the glasses. Then pour half of the lemon juice mixture into each glass and stir to combine with the liquor. Let the contents of the glasses rest for a few seconds until perfectly still, and then slowly pour 4 ounces of cola on top to get that half-and-half Arnold Palmer look.

THE DIRTY DUDETINI

||||||||||||||||||||||||||||||||||||||||||||||||||||||||||||||||||||||||||||||||||||||||||||||||||||||||||||||||||||||||||||

Martinis used to be cool. Jackie Gleason, George Burns, Dean Martin, James Bond — all martini guys. I know, I sound like I'm a hundred years old, but I challenge you to name one cool person who's ever ordered an appletini. I'm not even going to wait for an answer, because I know there isn't one. The world is aching for martinis to be cool again. Here's my offering.

Makes 1 cocktail

> 2 fluid ounces gin
> 1 tablespoon dry vermouth
> 1 tablespoon Crazy Shit Vinegar (see recipe, page 194)
> 1 slice pickled jalapeno, for garnish (optional; see Tip, page 195)
> 1 slice pickled carrot, for garnish (optional; see Tip, page 195)

Place your martini glass in the freezer. Fill a cocktail shaker with ice, and add the gin, vermouth, and vinegar. Stir with a long-handled spoon for 30 seconds. Remove the glass from the freezer, strain the contents of the shaker into the glass, and add the jalapeno and carrot garnishes, if using.

THE KNUCKLEHEAD

You probably could have guessed that I'm a huge Three Stooges fan. I watched their show as a kid, and I still watch it today. The Stooges were comic geniuses, dynamic performers, and true originals. When I needed names for this cocktail and the next one, I turned to my boys for inspiration.

Makes 1 cocktail

3 thin slices cucumber
4 or 5 mint leaves
1 lime wedge
4 or 5 ice cubes
1 shot (1½ fluid ounces) gin
6 fluid ounces tonic water

Place the cucumber and mint in the bottom of a highball glass, and smash them together with a muddler or the handle of a wooden spoon for 5 seconds. Squeeze the juice from the lime wedge over the crushed cucumber and mint, add the ice, gin, and tonic, and give it a stir. Drop in the squeezed lime wedge for good measure, and consume.

THE NUMBSKULL

IIIIIIIIIIIIIIIIIIIIIIIIIIIIIIIIIIIIIIIIIIIIIIIIIIIIIIIIIIIIIIIIIIIIIIIIIIIIIIIIIIIIIIIIIIIIIIIIIIIIIIIIIIIIIIIIIIIIIIIII

This is basically a margarita made from scratch, but I make a hibiscus-infused syrup to take the place of the sugar or simple syrup. You can find the dried hibiscus flowers in Mexican markets or on the interwebs. You can also put this delightful hibiscus syrup on other stuff that gets syrup, like pancakes.

Makes 4 cocktails

4 shots (6 fluid ounces) white tequila
½ cup fresh lime juice
½ cup triple sec
½ cup Hibiscus Syrup (recipe follows)
4 cups ice cubes
Lime Zest Salt (recipe follows)
1 lime wedge

In a blender, combine the tequila, lime juice, triple sec, hibiscus syrup, and ice, and blend on high until the mixture is slushy. Spread out the lime zest salt on a small plate. Rub the lime wedge along the rims of 4 margarita or rocks glasses to moisten them, then rub the rims of the glasses in the lime zest salt to coat them. Pour the frozen drink into the glasses, and try not to give yourself brain freeze.

HIBISCUS SYRUP

Store your extra syrup in a tightly closed mason jar in the fridge. It will last at least 4 months.

Makes 3 cups

2 cups water
½ cup dried hibiscus flowers
4 cups unrefined granulated sugar

In a nonreactive pot (like stainless steel or enamel), bring the water to a boil. Turn off the heat and add the hibiscus. Let the hibiscus steep for 25 minutes, then strain the mixture into another pot, pressing the hibiscus to extract all the liquid. (Now you have hibiscus tea. If you let it cool, slightly sweeten it, and pour it over ice, it makes a refreshing beverage on its own.) Add the sugar and bring the mixture to a boil, stirring until the sugar dissolves. Let it cool to room temperature before using.

LIME ZEST SALT

Store your extra lime zest salt in an airtight container at room temperature. It will last at least 6 months.

Makes 1 cup

1 cup kosher or sea salt
Zest of three limes

In a food processor, pulse the salt and zest until finely ground and fully combined.

THE GET BUSY

Turn to the person next to you, and ask them if they want one.

Makes 6 cocktails

1 cup roughly chopped strawberries
2 tablespoons unrefined granulated sugar
2 tablespoons fresh lemon juice
One 750 ml bottle champagne, sparkling wine, or prosecco
High-quality dark chocolate (optional)

Place the strawberries, sugar, and lemon juice in a bowl and mix well. This is called macerating (that's ma-CER-ating, people), which draws out the strawberries' natural sugars. Cover and refrigerate for 1 hour. Then, in a blender or food processor, puree the mixture. You can strain the puree through cheesecloth if you want to remove some of the seeds, but I personally don't mind them. Pour 4 ounces of champagne into each of the 6 glasses and, with a long-handled spoon, gently stir 1 tablespoon of the strawberry puree into each glass. (Any extra puree will be great in your morning smoothie.) Serve with the dark chocolate. Then have sex, either with yourself or with whoever else is there (as long as they're into it).

CHAPTER 2

Beatin' the Meat

meat substitutes

Q: What do you call a roomful of vegan dudes?
A: A soysage party.

IF YOU WERE BORN IN THE USA during the past century, you were born into a culture of meat. If you weren't born during the past hundred years, then you're either astonishingly old or from the future…and in either of these cases, I've got some questions. But let's say you were born in the twentieth century. Your parents were most likely not vegetarian or vegan, and there was probably even some semi-digested cheeseburger hanging out in your umbilical cord when it was cut (actually, I'm not sure if umbilical cords work that way — just roll with it). You grew up knowing meat as "the thing that goes in the middle of the plate." It may have been surrounded by veggies, or a grain, or, in my case, cheese, dough, and sauce, but no matter what, it was always there. How it came to be the centerpiece of our diets is debatable. But whether you believe it arrived out of necessity or through really, really good brainwa— er, um, I mean marketing, all that matters now is that you're reading this book. You have decided to reduce or eliminate your meat consumption, and that is fantastic! There may be times, especially when you're a new vegan, that you'll be jonesin' like a crackhead for some good old-fashioned spaghetti and meatballs, a mile-high deli sando, or some smoky bacon strips. Well, allow me to take care of those phantom itches and show you a few easy and delicious things to put where the meat used to go.

BASIC SEITAN

||||||||||||||||||||||||||||||||||||||||||||||||||||||||||||||||||||||||||||||||||||||||||||||||||||||||||||||||||||||||||||||||||||||

There are exactly 304,717.82 ways to make seitan, and here's one of them. It's simple, it's versatile, it's delicious, and it's a perfect intro to the world of seitan. Master it. Once you get the technique down and see how to cook and flavor seitan, you'll find the possibilities are as endless as the number of digits in pi. I must say that the tenderness is a result of adding mashed potatoes to the mix, a stroke of pure genius on my part. Yes, I just called myself a genius. You can slice this seitan for sandwiches, grind it for tacos, or make it into cutlets and strips for grilling. You can also chill it and place it on your eye after getting busted up in an underground bare-knuckled boxing match.

Makes 1 pound

½ pound russet potatoes, peeled and quartered
1 cup vital wheat gluten flour (see WTF below)
1 tablespoon chickpea flour or all-purpose flour
2 tablespoons Seitan Seasoning (see recipe, page 208)
⅓ cup low-sodium tamari or soy sauce (see WTF, next page)
½ teaspoon vegan Worcestershire sauce (see WTF, page 12)
⅓ cup plus 2 tablespoons water
¾ cup drained freshly cooked or rinsed canned white beans
     (cannellini, navy, etc.)

In a small pot, cover the potatoes with cold water, and bring to a boil. Boil for 8 to 10 minutes, or until the chunks easily fall apart when you put a fork through them. Drain the potatoes well and, while they're still hot, gently mash with a fork until there are no chunks left, or pass through a potato ricer. Set aside to cool. In a medium bowl, whisk together the wheat gluten, chickpea flour, and seitan seasoning.

WTF is vital wheat gluten?

It is the natural protein found in wheat. Making seitan from scratch appears to be an enormous pain in the ass, and I will never, ever do it. What I call for in this book is vital wheat gluten flour. You can get it at any health food store or on the interwebs.

In a food processor or blender, puree the tamari, Worcestershire, water, and beans. When the potatoes are cool enough to handle, add them and the bean mixture to the bowl with the dry ingredients, and mash it all together with your hands to form a soft dough, making sure there are no dry parts remaining. Let the dough rest at room temperature for 10 minutes before using. You can also wrap the dough in plastic and store it in the refrigerator for later use. It will last for 5 days.

- ### Seitan Slices (for sandwiches)

Scan to watch the video.

Shape the dough into a 2½-inch-diameter log. Wrap it loosely in foil (it will need space to expand during cooking), making sure the packet's completely sealed. Using a steamer basket, steam the seitan for 1 hour, then remove the foil, and let cool to room temperature. Then, for easier slicing, you can place it in the freezer for about 30 minutes until firm. You'll be able to get thinner slices this way. Store the slices in a zip-top bag for up to a week.

- ### Seitan Cutlets (great for grilling, chopping up for salads, or stir-fries)

Divide the dough into six portions. Flatten the portions on a cutting board with a rolling pin or your hand until they are an oblong shape, 3 to 4 inches long, 2 to 3 inches wide, and ¼ inch thick. Place a cutlet on a 12-by-12-inch square of foil. Leaving some space for expansion, loosely fold the sides of the foil over the dough, forming a flat packet. There is no need to twist or seal the ends of the foil. Repeat until you have six foil packets. Place one packet on top of another one, and repeat until you have three stacks of two packets. Take each stack and wrap the two packets together in another piece of foil, again leaving space for expansion, but this time crimp the edges of the foil together to seal the packets. So now you have three packets containing two cutlets each. Using a steamer basket, steam the cutlets for 1 hour, then remove and let cool to room temperature. Now you can do with them what you please... within the letter of the law, of course.

Scan to watch the video.

MY BALLS

||||||||||||||||||||||||||||||||||||||||||||||||||||||||||||||||||||||||||||||||||||||||||||||||||||||||||||||||||||

Here they are! For the whole planet to behold...My Balls! You can place them atop a pile of spaghetti or line them up in a hoagie roll, smother them with to-mato sauce and your favorite vegan cheese, and bake for a killer ball-parm sando.

Makes 10 to 12 balls

4 ounces tempeh
½ cup raw walnuts
1 tablespoon nutritional yeast (see WTF, next page)
1 teaspoon minced fresh Italian parsley
¼ teaspoon dried oregano
¼ teaspoon dried basil
¼ teaspoon dried thyme
2 cloves garlic, roughly chopped
¼ cup diced yellow onion
½ teaspoon vegan Worcestershire sauce (see WTF, page 12)
1 tablespoon tomato paste
1 teaspoon low-sodium tamari or soy sauce (see WTF, page 25)
1 tablespoon water
1 tablespoon extra-virgin olive oil, plus more to lube the
    baking sheet and coat the balls
Salt and pepper

Preheat the oven to 350°F. Using a steamer basket, steam the tem-peh for 25 minutes to soften it. Then let it cool. In a food proces-sor, combine the walnuts, nutritional yeast, parsley, oregano, basil, thyme, garlic, onion, Worcestershire, tomato paste, tamari, water, and oil, and process until you have a semi-moist meal.

In a bowl, crumble the steamed tempeh with your hands until there are no big chunks left. Then add the mixture from the food processor to the bowl, plus a pinch of salt and a grind of pepper, and mash it all together with your hands. You will now be able to form this mass into little balls. Make them just a bit smaller than beer-pong balls (depending on when and where you went to college, you may know them as Ping-Pong balls), about 1½ inches in diameter.

Lube up a baking sheet with the oil, lay the balls on it, coat them with a little more oil, and bake for 30 minutes. My balls are now ready for consumption.

WTF is nutritional yeast?
It's a yellow, flaky, nutty, cheesy-tasting substance. It's made by culturing stuff, and other natural science-y processes that I don't care to learn about. All I care about is that it's a great source of vitamin B_{12} and deliciousness, so I use it a lot. Find it in the supplement or bulk section of a health food store, or on the interwebs.

PRETEND ITALIAN SAUSAGES

||||||||||||||||||||||||||||||||||||||||||||||||||||||||||||||||||||||||||||||||||||||||||||||||||||||||||||||||||||||||||||||||||||||||||

Toss these with some Tomato Killer and sauteed peppers and onions, and throw them on a crusty Italian roll. Classic.

Makes 8 sausages

½ pound russet potatoes, peeled and quartered
1 cup vital wheat gluten flour (see WTF, page 24)
2 tablespoons Seitan Seasoning (see recipe, page 208)
¼ teaspoon chili flakes
½ teaspoon fennel seeds
1 tablespoon chickpea flour or all-purpose flour
¼ cup low-sodium tamari or soy sauce (see WTF, page 25)
¾ cup water
¼ cup diced yellow onion
3 cloves garlic, roughly chopped
1 tablespoon chopped oil-packed sun-dried tomatoes
½ cup drained freshly cooked or rinsed canned white beans
   (cannellini, navy, etc.)
Extra-virgin olive oil (optional)

In a small pot, cover the potatoes with cold water, and bring to a boil. Boil for 8 to 10 minutes, or until the chunks easily fall apart when you put a fork through them. Drain the potatoes well and, while they're still hot, gently mash with a fork until there are no chunks left, or pass through a potato ricer. Set aside to cool.

In a bowl, whisk together the wheat gluten, seitan seasoning, chili flakes, fennel seeds, and chickpea flour. In a food processor or blender, puree the tamari, water, onion, garlic, sun-dried tomatoes, and beans. When the potatoes are cool enough to handle, add them and the bean mixture to the bowl with the dry ingredients, and mash it all together with your hands to form a soft dough, making sure there are no dry parts remaining. Let the dough rest for 10 minutes before using. You can also wrap it in plastic and store it in the refrigerator for later use. It will last for 5 days.

Form the dough into a loaf-like shape and cut it in half. Then cut those halves in half. Finally, cut the halves of the halves into five-sixteenths…just kidding, cut them in half. Now you'll have 8 portions. Roll them into cigar-like shapes, 4 inches long and ½ inch wide. Loosely roll each portion in foil and twist the ends of the foil to seal the packet. Remember to leave some room for expansion. Using a steamer basket, steam for 1 hour. If you want crispier outsides, after the sausages have steamed, fry them in a skillet or grill them with a little olive oil for a couple of minutes, until browned.

Scan to watch the video.

VARIATION: Pretend Chipotle Sausages

Omit the chili flakes and add 1 or 2 chipotle peppers (depending on how hot you like it) to the food processor or blender before you puree the wet ingredients.

PRETEND BREAKFAST SAUSAGE PATTIES

The answer is yes, I'm a fan of sausage.

Makes 8 to 10 patties

1 cup cooked green lentils, drained
1 tablespoon grated yellow onion
1 clove garlic, minced
1 teaspoon maple syrup
½ cup vital wheat gluten flour (see WTF, page 24)
¼ teaspoon vegetable bouillon powder
Pinch of chili flakes
½ teaspoon fennel seeds
1 teaspoon nutritional yeast (see WTF, page 27)
¼ teaspoon paprika
¼ teaspoon salt
Pepper
½ cup water
2 teaspoons extra-virgin olive oil

In a large bowl, combine the lentils, onion, garlic, maple syrup, wheat gluten, bouillon powder, chili flakes, fennel seeds, nutritional yeast, paprika, salt, and a pinch of pepper. Mash it all together with your hands, then slowly add the water (you may not need all of it), continuing to mash, until it becomes a soft yet somewhat stretchy dough. Make sure there are no clumps of dry wheat gluten. Form the dough into a 2-inch-diameter log and wrap tightly in foil. In a steamer basket, steam for 1 hour.

TIP

Uncooked patties freeze very well in a zip-top bag, and they can go straight from the freezer into the frying pan; in that case, just cook them for a few extra minutes.

When the steaming is complete, remove the foil and let the sausage cool to room temperature. When it's cool, slice it into 8 to 10 patties.

In a pan, heat the oil over medium-high heat, then add your sausage patties (do it in batches if you need to). Cook for 3 to 4 minutes per side, or until they're browned, then serve.

TEMPEH BACON

|||||||||||||||||||||||||||||||||||||||||||||||||||||||||||||||||||||||||||||||||||||||||||||||||||||||||

Because you deserve it.

Makes about 16 strips

½ cup low-sodium tamari or soy sauce (see WTF, page 25)
1½ tablespoons Crazy Shit Vinegar (see recipe, page 194) or
    apple cider vinegar
1 teaspoon garlic powder
1 teaspoon paprika
2 teaspoons molasses
2 teaspoons vegan Worcestershire sauce (see WTF, page 12)
1 drop liquid smoke (see WTF below)
Pepper
One 8-ounce package tempeh, sliced into ⅛-inch-thick strips
Extra-virgin olive oil for frying (optional)

In a medium bowl, whisk together the tamari, vinegar, garlic pow-der, paprika, molasses, Worcestershire, liquid smoke, and a cou-ple grinds of pepper. Pour the marinade into a zip-top bag, add the tempeh slices, gently slosh them around so they get coated, squeeze the bag to suck out as much of the air as possible, and zip it closed. Put the bag in the fridge to let the tempeh marinate for at least 8 hours (24 hours is ideal).

WTF is liquid smoke?

Liquid smoke (a.k.a. *hickory seasoning*) can
be found at just about any grocery store
near the ketchup and barbecue sauces. It
is very strong and a small bottle will
last a long time.

Scan to watch the video.

To cook the bacon, let any excess marinade fall away from the strips, and either bake at 375°F for about 10 minutes or fry in a pan with a little oil over medium heat for about 3 minutes per side, until browned.

TIP

I highly recommend making extra tempeh bacon as it freezes very well. Place a piece of parchment paper on a plate or baking sheet that will fit in your freezer. Let any excess marinade fall away from your uncooked bacon strips and place them on the parchment so they don't touch each other. Place them in the freezer, uncovered, for an hour. They should be pretty solid at this point, so transfer them to a zip-top bag, and they'll be good for at least a month in the freezer.

PRETEND CANADIAN BACON

|||||||||||||||||||||||||||||||||||||||||||||||||||||||||||||||||||||||||||||||||||||||||||||||||||

This one's for my Canadian cohorts, who give me all kinds of love. I know that many people hold a high regard for those who have been knighted by the Queen of England. Personally I'd prefer to be "Mountied".

Makes 12 slices

One 16-ounce block super-firm tofu (or one 14-ounce block very-well-drained extra-firm tofu; see Tip below and Tip on next page)
½ cup low-sodium tamari or soy sauce (see WTF, page 25)
1 teaspoon liquid smoke (see WTF, page 32)
½ cup maple syrup
1 tablespoon smoked paprika
½ teaspoon garlic powder
¼ teaspoon pepper
1 tablespoon extra-virgin olive oil

Cut the block of tofu into 2-by-3-inch pieces. Then cut the pieces into ⅛-inch-thick slices. (If you want to get fancy, you can use a round cookie cutter or pint glass to cut circular slices, but that will leave excess that will go to waste.)

In a small bowl, whisk together the tamari, liquid smoke, maple syrup, paprika, garlic powder, and pepper. Pour the mixture into a large zip-top bag, add the tofu slices, gently slosh them around so they get coated, squeeze the bag to

TIP

Super-firm tofu has the least amount of water of all the tofus. This allows it to hold together very well for grilling or broiling. When very well drained, some extra-firm tofu can get pretty close to the texture of the super-firm tofu, so it's a manageable substitute.

suck out as much of the air as possible, and place the bag in the fridge to let the tofu marinate for at least 3 hours but no more than 5 hours.

In a large skillet, heat the oil over high heat. Place as many slices as you wish (without overcrowding) into the hot pan, and fry until browned on one side (3 to 4 minutes), then flip and repeat. Cook the bacon in batches if you need to. If you would like to freeze the uncooked slices, use the same freezing method as with the Tempeh Bacon (see recipe, page 32) to preserve these for up to a month.

TIP
Drain that tofu!!

There's a ton of water in that block, and we have no use for it. Take the block out of the water it's packed in, and place it on a plate. Then put another plate on top of it and add something heavy on top of that plate, like a couple of cans of beans. Let it drain for 30 to 60 minutes — the longer, the better. Discard the water and proceed with your preparations.

TEMPEH CHORIZO

||||||||||||||||||||||||||||||||||||||||||||||||||||||||||||||||||||||||||||||||||||||||||||||||||||||||||||||||||||||||||||||||||||||

This ground Mexican sausage is great for taquitos, burritos, and breakfast scrambles. It's also great if you don't like making out with other humans. Potent stuff.

Makes 2 cups

One 8-ounce package tempeh
4 cloves garlic, grated
1 teaspoon cumin seeds (or ½ teaspoon ground cumin)
¼ teaspoon ground cloves
½ teaspoon ground coriander
1 tablespoon smoked paprika
2 teaspoons dried oregano
2 tablespoons chili powder
Pinch of cinnamon
Salt and pepper
2 teaspoons extra-virgin olive oil
1 tablespoon sherry vinegar
1 cup vegetable stock

In a large bowl, combine the tempeh, garlic, cumin, cloves, coriander, paprika, oregano, chili powder, cinnamon, a pinch of salt, and a pinch of pepper. With a fork, potato masher, or your very clean hands, mash everything together until the tempeh is completely "ground" and coated in the spices. Heat the olive oil in a large skillet over medium heat, and add the tempeh mixture. Cook until it gets a bit browned, 5 to 7 minutes. Add the vinegar and cook for 1 minute, then stir in the vegetable stock. Cover and simmer over medium heat, 4 to 5 more minutes, or until the liquid is almost absorbed. Season with salt and pepper to taste.

CHAPTER 3
The Second Most Important Meal of the Day, after Cocktails

breakfast

IF YOU'RE ONE OF THOSE PEOPLE who like to have a light breakfast like a slice of toast, a piece of fruit, a bowl of cereal, or a carafe of coffee, then this chapter is definitely not for you. These dishes are hearty and filling. They will make you a Saturday-morning god in the bloodshot eyes of your passed-out-on-the-couch friends. They will elevate you to royalty at Sunday brunch. And they will make you a Casanova when served to someone in bed, thus guaranteeing additional Caligula-like activities. Mastering these breakfast recipes will help you earn your official "Stamp of Awesome."

MOSTEST ULTIMATE-EST BREAKFAST SANDWICH
IN THE HISTORY OF THE UNIVERSE

I think the title of this one is introduction enough.

Makes 4 sandwiches

4 teaspoons extra-virgin olive oil
2 tablespoons Scramble Seasoning (see recipe, page 209)
Four 3-by-3-by-¼-inch slices drained
    extra-firm tofu (see Tip, page 35)
4 teaspoons vegan mayo (see WTF below)
4 English muffins, halved and toasted
8 strips Tempeh Bacon (see recipe, page 32), fully prepared
    and kept warm
4 Pretend Breakfast Sausage Patties (see recipe, page 30),
    fully prepared and kept warm
1 packed cup mixed greens (like baby romaine, arugula,
    radicchio, and mesclun)
4 slices beefsteak tomato
Salt and pepper

WTF is vegan mayo?

It is something I have not been able to
replicate using household ingredients.
A company called Follow Your Heart makes
my favorite one, Vegenaise. It's made with
grapeseed oil, and it's delicious. You can get it
at any health food store or on the interwebs.

In a medium skillet, heat the oil over medium-high heat. Spread out the scramble seasoning on a plate, pat the tofu dry, and dredge both sides of each slice in the seasoning. When the oil in the pan is hot, carefully add your tofu slices. Cook, without moving the tofu, for 4 to 5 minutes, or until browned on one side. Flip and cook the other side for 4 to 5 minutes, or until browned.

Spread ½ teaspoon mayo on each toasted muffin half and assemble sandwiches from the bottom up in the following order: 1 muffin half, 2 strips of tempeh bacon, 1 slice of tofu, 1 sausage patty, ¼ cup of greens, 1 slice of tomato, salt and pepper, another muffin half. Eat.

HANGOVER HASH

||||||||||||||||||||||||||||||||||||||||||||||||||||||||||||||||||||||||||||||||||||||||||||||||||||||||||||

You know that nonsensical urge to eat something fried, greasy, and generally unhealthful whilst in the throes of a severe hangover? Well, Hangover Hash will satisfy that urge while not being at all greasy and providing you with plenty of nutrition. I also find it goes great with a Bloodbath (see recipe, page 12)...just sayin'.

Serves 4

½ cup quinoa, rinsed thoroughly (see Tip, next page)
Water
Salt
2 large russet potatoes, peeled and diced
4 teaspoons extra-virgin olive oil
1 teaspoon smoked paprika
Pepper
1 cup thinly sliced leek
1 cup diced red bell pepper
4 cups sliced cremini mushrooms
8 Pretend Breakfast Sausage Patties (see recipe, page 30),
    fully prepared and roughly chopped
2 tablespoons minced fresh Italian parsley

In a small pot, cover the quinoa with 1 cup of water and add a pinch of salt. Bring to a boil, then lower the heat and let simmer, covered, for 10 to 12 minutes, or until the quinoa is soft and the water is completely absorbed. Spread it out on a wide pan or plate so that it cools quickly and doesn't overcook. Set aside.

In another small pot, cover the potato with cold water and bring to a boil. Boil until fork-tender, 4 to 6 minutes. Drain and let drip-dry in a colander for 2 to 3 minutes. In a medium bowl, toss the potatoes in 2 teaspoons of the oil, the paprika, and salt and pepper.

In a large pan or skillet, heat the remaining 2 teaspoons of oil over medium-high heat. Add the leek, bell pepper, mushrooms, and a pinch of salt. Cook for 4 to 5 minutes, then push them off to the side to make room for the potatoes. Add the seasoned potatoes to the pan and let them brown for 2 to 3 minutes, without stirring. Carefully flip the potatoes and let them brown on the other side for 2 more minutes. Add the quinoa, sausage, parsley, and salt and pepper to taste, and stir until evenly combined. Gently press the hash into an even layer with the back of a spatula. Let it brown on this side for about 2 minutes, then divvy it up into 4 portions and scarf it down.

TIP
Rinse that quinoa!
Using a fine-mesh strainer, rinse the quinoa until the water runs clear. This will remove the bitterness of the grain.

SEXY'S SCRAMBLE

||||||||||||||||||||||||||||||||||||||||||||||||||||||||||||||||||||||||||||||||||||||||||||||||||||||||||||||||||||||||||||||

A great, high-protein breakfast that can be the answer to the seemingly ubiquitous question, "So where do you get your protein?"

Serves 4

2 tablespoons extra-virgin olive oil
1 cup thinly sliced scallions
1 cup diced red bell pepper
Salt
4 cloves garlic, chopped
Two 14-ounce blocks extra-firm tofu, drained (see Tip, page 35)
4 tablespoons Scramble Seasoning (see recipe, page 209)
4 Roma tomatoes, diced
2 cups drained freshly cooked or rinsed canned black beans
1 cup fresh or thawed frozen corn kernels
1 cup Not Yo Mama's Cheeze Sauce (optional; see recipe, page 216)
1 avocado, thinly sliced
Eight 6-inch corn tortillas, warmed

In a large skillet, heat the oil over medium-high heat. Add the scallions, bell pepper, and a pinch of salt. Saute for 2 to 3 minutes. Add the garlic and cook for 2 more minutes. Crumble the drained tofu into a scramble-esque texture, add it to the pan, and toss it with the scallions, bell pepper, and garlic. Let the tofu mixture cook on one side for 4 or 5 minutes — and don't you dare touch it. We're trying to get some brownage, without stickage, so you must leave it be.

Now that you've obeyed my commands, stir in the scramble seasoning, and let the mixture cook for 2 to 3 more minutes. Stir in the tomatoes, beans, corn, and cheeze sauce, and cook for 3 more minutes, until all ingredients are warmed through. Pile it up on a serving plate, top it with the sliced avocado, and serve it with the warmed corn tortillas.

MORNING BENEDICTION

As a member of the clergy (see episode #18), I feel it is my Internet-given right to bless you with this glorious offering.

Serves 4

Scan to watch the video.

½ cup Hollandaze Sauce (see recipe, page 212)
4 teaspoons extra-virgin olive oil
2 tablespoons Scramble Seasoning (see recipe, page 209)
Four 3-by-3-by-¼-inch-thick slices drained extra-firm tofu (see Tip, page 35)
2 English muffins, halved and toasted
Vegan margarine for muffin slathering
4 slices Pretend Canadian Bacon (see recipe, page 34), fully prepared and kept warm
4 thick slices beefsteak tomato
4 sprigs fresh parsley, for garnish (optional)

In a small pot, gently heat the Hollandaze Sauce over low heat. In a medium skillet, heat the oil over medium-high heat. Spread out the scramble seasoning on a plate, pat the tofu dry, and dredge both sides of each slice in the seasoning. When the oil in the pan is hot, carefully add your tofu slices. Cook, without moving the tofu, for 4 to 5 minutes, or until browned on one side. Flip and cook the other side for 4 to 5 minutes, or until browned.

Set the toasted English muffin halves on 4 separate plates. Slather them with margarine, and top each half with 1 slice of Canadian Bacon, 1 slice of tomato, and 1 slice of tofu. Artfully drizzle the hollandaze sauce over the top. Garnish each serving with a parsley sprig.

AVOCADO TOAST

||||||||||||||||||||||||||||||||||||||||||||||||||||||||||||||||||||||||||||||||||||||||||||||||||||||||||||||

Avocado. Toast. How could this be bad, right?

Serves 4

2 avocados, diced
1 teaspoon extra-virgin olive oil
1 teaspoon your favorite hot sauce
Salt and pepper
4 slices bread, toasted
8 strips Tempeh Bacon (see recipe, page 32), fully prepared
    and kept warm
12 thin slices tomato

In a bowl, combine the avocados, olive oil, and hot sauce. Fold the ingredients together, mashing the avocados slightly, and season with salt and pepper to taste. Spread the avocado mixture evenly on the toasted bread, and top each slice with 2 strips of tempeh bacon and 3 slices of tomato. Sprinkle more salt and pepper on the tomatoes, and serve.

THE BIG ONE

|||||||||||||||||||||||||||||||||||||||||||||||||||||||||||||||||||||||||||||||||||||||||||||||||||||||||||||||||||||||||||

Don't make any plans for the afternoon, because this breakfast burrito is going to put you right back in bed.

Makes 4 burritos

1 medium russet potato, peeled and diced
1 tablespoon olive oil
½ cup thinly sliced scallions
½ cup diced red bell pepper
Salt
One 14-ounce block extra-firm tofu, drained (see Tip, page 35)
2 tablespoons Scramble Seasoning (see recipe, page 209)
2 packed cups baby spinach
2 cups Tempeh Chorizo (see recipe, page 36), fully prepared
Four 12-inch flour tortillas, warmed
1 cup Not Yo Mama's Cheeze Sauce (see recipe, page 216) or other vegan cheese
2 medium avocados, thinly sliced
2 medium Roma tomatoes, diced
Pepper

In a small pot, cover the potato with cold water and bring to a boil. Boil until fork-tender, about 6 minutes. Drain and let drip-dry in a colander for 2 to 3 minutes. Set aside. In a large skillet, heat the oil over medium-high heat. Add the scallions, bell pepper, potato, and a pinch of salt, and saute for 4 to 5 minutes, until the potato begins to brown. Crumble the drained tofu into a scramble-esque texture, add it to the pan, and toss. Let the tofu mixture cook on one side for 4 to 5 minutes, or until it begins to brown. Add the scramble seasoning, and toss everything together. Let it cook for 3 to 4 more minutes, then stir in the spinach and the tempeh chorizo. Cook until the spinach is wilted and the chorizo is warmed through, about 4 more minutes, then remove from the heat.

Lay out one warmed tortilla, and as you look at it, imagine you're looking at a compass. The fillings should be placed halfway between the midpoint and the southern end of the tortilla. First spread out about one-quarter of the cheeze sauce, then add one-quarter of the tofu-chorizo mixture, and top that with one-quarter of the avocado and tomato. Fold in the east and west sides of the tortilla first. Then roll the southern end northward. Repeat with the remaining ingredients to make 4 burritos.

THE REAL MAN'S QUICHE

||||||||||||||||||||||||||||||||||||||||||||||||||||||||||||||||||||||||||||||||||||||||||||||||||

"Real men don't eat quiche," you say? I say, look at the name of this dish — clearly they do. Duh.

Serves 4

1 tablespoon plus 1 teaspoon extra-virgin olive oil
½ cup diced yellow onion
Salt
3 cloves garlic, minced (see Tip, next page)
¼ pound cremini mushrooms, sliced
4 packed cups baby spinach
One 14-ounce block extra-firm tofu, drained
    (see Tip, page 35)
⅔ cup unsweetened soy milk
½ teaspoon Dijon mustard
2 tablespoons Scramble Seasoning (see recipe, page 209)
¼ teaspoon chili flakes
2 tablespoons minced fresh Italian parsley, plus more for garnish
6 strips Tempeh Bacon (see recipe, page 32), fully prepared
    and roughly chopped
4 Pretend Breakfast Sausage Patties (see recipe, page 30),
    fully prepared and diced
¼ teaspoon paprika

Preheat the oven to 375°F. In a large skillet, heat the 1 tablespoon of oil over medium-high heat. Add the onion and a pinch of salt, and saute for 3 minutes. Then add the garlic and cook for 1 minute. Next, add the mushrooms and cook for 4 minutes. Finally, add the spinach and cook until it's wilted, about 2 minutes. Remove from the heat.

Break the tofu into manageable chunks and put it in a food processor along with the soy milk, mustard, scramble seasoning, chili flakes, and parsley. Process until smooth.

In a large bowl, combine the tofu mixture, shroom mixture, tempeh bacon, and sausage patties, and stir until well mixed. Use the remaining 1 teaspoon of olive oil to lube up a 5-by-7-inch casserole dish. Add the tofu mixture to the dish, spread it out evenly, and sprinkle the top with the paprika. Bake uncovered for 40 to 50 minutes, or until quiche is set. If you desire a browner top, broil it for 1 to 2 minutes after you take it out of the oven. Garnish with parsley, and let it hang out for 5 minutes before you cut it.

TIP

The way you cut up your garlic makes a difference. Mincing makes it more potent, and it can burn in the pan quickly, while slicing it gives it a milder flavor and also allows for it to get slightly toasted without burning, which gives it a nice flavor. I'm sure these facts have something to do with science, but that's about all I can tell you.

SAILOR'S OATMEAL WITH GLAZED WALNUTS

||||||||||||||||||||||||||||||||||||||||||||||||||||||||||||||||||||||||||||||||||||||||||||||||||||||||||||||

I like rum...and Sailor Jerry rum rules all! Making it into a syrup brings out Sailor Jerry's inherent sweetness, making it a uniquely delicious sweetener for any number of dishes, from ice cream to oatmeal.

Serves 4

2 cups raw walnuts
¾ cup Sailor Syrup (recipe follows)
2 cups rolled oats
1 teaspoon salt
6 to 8 cups water (8 if you like it creamy, 6 if you like it thick)
½ cup diced dried apricots

Preheat the oven to 350°F. In a baking dish, add the walnuts and pour ¼ cup of the sailor syrup over them. Toss until evenly coated, and bake for 5 to 7 minutes, until browned. Remove from the oven and let cool completely before using.

In a large pot, combine the oats, salt, and water, and bring to a boil. Then turn down to simmer, stirring occasionally. Cook until the oatmeal reaches the desired consistency (thick or creamy), about 10 minutes. Stir in up to ½ cup of the remaining sailor syrup, or until it's sufficiently sweet. Transfer the oatmeal to 4 bowls, and top with apricots and glazed walnuts.

SAILOR SYRUP

Store your extra syrup in a tightly closed mason jar in the fridge. It will last at least 4 months.

Makes 3 cups

4 cups Sailor Jerry rum
4 cups unrefined granulated sugar

In a medium pot, bring the rum to a simmer over medium-high heat. Continue simmering until the rum is reduced by half. Add the sugar, and stir until it dissolves. Turn off the heat, and let the syrup cool to room temperature.

THE ALMOND BROTHERS BREAKFAST BAR

|||||||||||||||||||||||||||||||||||||||||||||||||||||||||||||||||||||||||||||||||||||||||||||||||||||||||||||||||

Jam out a batch of these on Sunday, and you can groove to work all week with one in your hand. Righteous.

Makes 12 bars

1 cup roughly chopped raw almonds
1 cup raw shelled sunflower seeds
¼ cup roasted pepitas (see WTF below)
1 cup rolled oats
8 ounces dried cherries
1 cup almond butter
¼ cup maple syrup
2 ripe bananas, mashed or passed through a potato ricer
Salt
Light oil or vegan margarine for greasing pan

Preheat the oven to 300°F. In a large bowl, combine the almonds, sunflower seeds, pepitas, oats, cherries, almond butter, maple syrup, bananas, and a pinch of salt, and stir until well mixed. Lube up a 9-by-13-inch baking dish with the oil, and pour in the nut mixture. Press the nut mixture all the way out to the edges, making sure it's in an even layer. Bake for 25 minutes, or until the edges are slightly brown. Remove from the oven, and let cool on the counter for at least 1 hour. Cut into bars by cutting crosswise into quarters, then lengthwise into thirds. Store the breakfast bars in a zip-top bag in the fridge for up to a week.

WTF is a pepita?

A pepita is the hulled and usually roasted kernel of a pumpkin seed. You can find pepitas in the Mexican aisle of most grocery stores. If you can only find raw pepitas, simply heat a medium skillet over medium-high heat and toss them in. No oil is needed. Allow them to slightly brown on each side, which should only take a minute or so. You can also roast them in a 350°F oven for 5 minutes. Let them cool, and they're ready to use.

SMOOTHNESS

||||||||||||||||||||||||||||||||||||||||||||||||||||||||||||||||||||||||||||||||||||||||||||||||||||||

I rock one of these at least 2 or 3 times per week. There are so many variations: strawberries, raspberries, mango, pineapple, snozberries…the choices are virtually endless.

Makes about two 2-cup servings

   2 ripe bananas, broken into thirds
   1 cup frozen or fresh berries or other fruit of your choice
   1 cup fresh orange juice
   2 cups nondairy milk (my favorite is almond milk)

In a blender, combine all the ingredients, and puree.

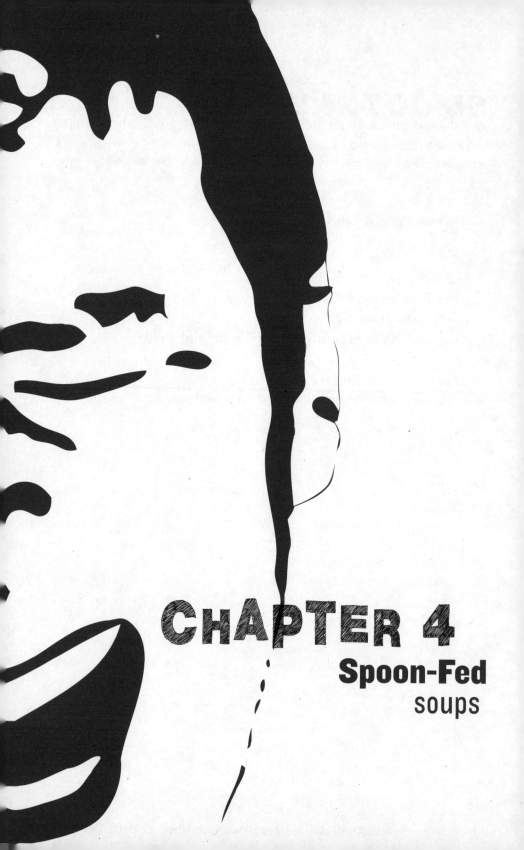

CHAPTER 4
Spoon-Fed
soups

SOUP IS MY FAVORITE FOOD. The Girlfriend says that I'm copying her because it's her favorite food too. I argue that early on in our relationship, when she said that soup was *her* favorite food, I remember thinking that it was nice, because it was my favorite food too. Since I didn't say it out loud at the time, however, she's not giving me credit for it being my favorite food first. I'm not even saying that it was my favorite food first, I don't really care all that much — but I do not want to be known as a favorite food copier. That I could not bear.

NEW ENGLAND BLAM CHOWDER

|||||||||||||||||||||||||||||||||||||||||||||||||||||||||||||||||||||||||||||||||||||||||||||||||||||||||

I cleverly change the C to a B and BLAM! We've got a delicious vegan chowder.

Serves 6 (6 cups)

1 cup whole raw cashews
2 teaspoons extra-virgin olive oil
1 cup diced yellow onion
1 cup thinly sliced carrot
1 cup thinly sliced celery
Salt
¼ pound oyster mushrooms, chopped (shiitake mushrooms
    work too)
1 teaspoon minced fresh thyme
1 bay leaf
1 cup white wine
1 cup diced red potatoes
4 cups vegetable stock
2 cups unsweetened almond milk
1 tablespoon nutritional yeast (see WTF, page 27)
1 tablespoon seaweed powder (see WTF, next page)
Pepper
6 strips Tempeh Bacon (see recipe, page 32), fully prepared
    and roughly chopped

In a small pot, cover the cashews with water and bring to a boil. Boil for 8 minutes, then drain and set aside. In a large pot, heat the oil over medium heat and add the onion, carrot, celery, and a pinch of salt. Cook for 3 to 4 minutes, stirring occasionally. Add the mushrooms, thyme, and bay leaf, and cook, stirring occasionally, for 3 to 4 more minutes. Add the wine, and simmer for 2 minutes.

Add the potatoes and stock, and continue simmering for about 10 more minutes.

Meanwhile, in a food processor, puree the boiled cashews, almond milk, and nutritional yeast until smooth, 2 to 3 minutes. Now that your potatoes are fork-tender, fish out the bay leaf and stir in the cashew cream and seaweed powder, then season with salt and pepper to taste. Sprinkle the tempeh bacon on top just before serving.

WTF is seaweed powder?

It's dried, ground-up seaweed that's a great source of vitamin B_{12}, calcium, minerals, iron, and iodine, and it makes things taste of the sea. Find it at health food stores or in the Asian section of your supermarket.

CAULIFLOWER AND ROASTED FENNEL SOUP

||||||||||||||||||||||||||||||||||||||||||||||||||||||||||||||||||||||||||||||||||||||||||||||||||||||||||||||||||||||||||||||||||||||||||||||||||||||

This is a favorite of our clients at Vegin' Out, so I had to share.

Serves 6 (6 cups)

1 head fennel

2 teaspoons extra-virgin olive oil, plus more for coating the fennel

Salt and pepper

1 cup diced yellow onion

4 cloves garlic, minced

1 russet potato, peeled and cut into 1-inch cubes

1 head cauliflower, cut into florets

3 cups vegetable stock

Preheat the oven to 350°F. Cut off the fennel stalks and cut them into ¼-inch pieces. Set aside. Cut the fennel bulb in half and coat each half with a little olive oil, and sprinkle with salt and pepper. On a baking sheet, roast the fennel bulb halves, cut side down, for 30 to 40 minutes, or until tender and browned. Remove from the oven, let cool, and cut into large chunks.

In a pot, heat the 2 teaspoons of oil to medium, and add the onion, sliced fennel stalks, and a healthy pinch of salt. Cook for 4 to 6 minutes, or until tender. Add the garlic and cook for 4 more minutes, then add the potato, cauliflower, and roasted fennel. Add the vegetable stock, bring to a simmer, and cook for 20 minutes, until the cauliflower and potatoes are very tender. Use a handheld blender or pour the soup into a food processor or blender, and puree until smooth. Season with salt and pepper to taste.

COUNTRY VEGGIE SOUP

||||||||||||||||||||||||||||||||||||||||||||||||||||||||||||||||||||||||||||||||||||||||||||||||||||||||||

This soup reminds me of my early days workin' down on the family farm. Tossing bales of hay with those big hook things from dawn till dusk gave me perspective and showed me what really mattered in life. It would be chilly in early spring, and a soup like this would warm my body and my soul. I just made all of that up. This soup rules!

Serves 6 (6 cups)

2 teaspoons extra-virgin olive oil
½ cup diced yellow onion
1 leek, halved lengthwise and sliced
½ cup diced carrot
2 stalks celery, sliced
Salt
½ cup diced red potatoes
4 cups vegetable stock
¾ cup cooked barley
1 large leaf Swiss chard, stemmed and roughly chopped
1 tablespoon chopped fresh Italian parsley
Pepper

In a medium pot, heat the oil over medium heat, and add the onion, leek, carrot, celery, and a pinch of salt. Cook the veggies for 5 to 7 minutes, or until softened. Add the potatoes and stock. Simmer until the potatoes are fork-tender, 8 to 10 minutes. Add the barley and chard, and simmer for 2 more minutes. Turn off the heat, stir in the parsley, season with salt and pepper to taste, and serve.

MINESTRONE

This is my favorite soup on the planet. The key to this one is the cabbage. You may be like, "Waahhh, waahhh, waahhh, I don't like cabbage! I'm a big baby! Waaaahhhh!" Well, I don't give a shit! You'll use it, and you'll like it.

Serves 4 (4 cups)

½ cup small elbow pasta or other small pasta
2 teaspoons extra-virgin olive oil
1 cup diced yellow onion
1 large leek, sliced
1 cup diced carrot
1 cup sliced celery
Salt
3 cloves garlic, minced
2 teaspoons tomato paste
One 15-ounce can diced tomatoes, with juice
2 cups vegetable stock
1½ cups thinly sliced green cabbage
2 cups drained freshly cooked white beans (cannellini, navy, etc.)
    or one 15-ounce can white beans, rinsed and drained
2 tablespoons finely chopped fresh Italian parsley
Pepper

Cook the pasta according to the directions on the package. When the pasta is al dente, drain, cool immediately under cold running water, and set aside in a colander to drain.

In a large pot, heat the oil over medium heat. Add the onion, leek, carrot, celery, and a healthy pinch of salt. Cook until soft, 3 to 5 minutes. Stir in the garlic, and cook for 3 to 4 more minutes. Stir in the tomato paste, and cook for 1 minute. Add the diced tomatoes (with juice) and vegetable stock, and simmer for 20 minutes. Add the cabbage and beans, and cook for 2 more minutes. Turn off the heat, and stir in the cooked pasta, parsley, and salt and pepper to taste.

ONION SOUP

||||||||||||||||||||||||||||||||||||||||||||||||||||||||||||||||||||||||||||||||||||||||||||||||||||||

This is probably my second favorite soup. My mom would always order onion soup when the family went out to eat; she loved it. I thought it looked totally gross, all brown and stringy. Blah. Then, for pretty much no reason at all, I would kick my brother under the table, causing a huge scene, and we'd have to get our check and leave the restaurant before she could finish her beloved soup. Ahhh... memories.

Serves 6 (6 cups)

1 tablespoon vegan margarine
2 pounds yellow onions, thinly sliced
Pinch of salt
3 cloves garlic, minced
2 teaspoons chopped fresh thyme
1 cup white wine
2 tablespoons vegan Worcestershire sauce (see WTF, page 12)
4 cups vegetable stock
2 teaspoons arrowroot dissolved in 1 teaspoon water (see WTF, next page)
Pepper
Six ¼-inch-thick baguette slices, toasted
6 tablespoons Not-zzarella Sauce (see recipe, page 214) or 6 slices other vegan cheeze

In a large pot, melt the margarine over medium heat. When it begins to sizzle a bit, add the onion and a healthy pinch of salt, and stir it all around. Let it cook for about 3 minutes without stirring, then add your garlic and do not stir. Let it continue cooking without stirring for 2 more minutes, then stir. Lower the heat to medium-low, and stir in the thyme.

After 20 more minutes (stirring every so often), the onions should be very soft and smell sweet. We're looking for caramelization, so they should be starting to brown a bit. Now is the time to add the wine…it's tough to part with, I know, but trust me on this one, you want it in there. Let the wine cook for 2 minutes, then stir in the Worcestershire. Cook for 1 more minute, then add the vegetable stock. Raise the heat to medium, cover, and simmer for 20 minutes. After this time has elapsed, stir in the arrowroot slurry, and cook for 1 more minute. Season with salt and pepper to taste.

Now it's ready to serve. Set your broiler on high. Divide the soup into ovenproof bowls or those fancy crock things, float a toasty baguette slice on each, and hit each one with 1 tablespoon of not-zzarella sauce or 1 slice of fake cheese. Put them under the broiler for 1 to 2 minutes, or until the cheese is melted or slightly browned. Now it's ready to eat. Let the tongue scalding begin!

WTF is arrowroot?

It's a plant-based thickening agent much like cornstarch. You simply dissolve it in a little water (this is called a slurry) and add as much as you need to a simmering soup or sauce until the soup or sauce reaches your desired thickness. Find it at a health food store or on the interwebs.

WHITE BEAN AND KALE SOUP

IIIIIIIIIIIIIIIIIIIIIIIIIIIIIIIIIIIIIIIIIIIIIIIIIIIIIIIIIIIIIIIIIIIIIIIIIIIIIIIIIIIIIIIIIIIIIIIIIIIIIIIIIIIIIIIIIIIIIIIIIIII

The rosemary in this soup really makes it. Please use fresh and not dried. Big difference.

Serves 6 (6 cups)

2 teaspoons extra-virgin olive oil
½ cup diced yellow onion
½ cup thinly sliced carrot
1 large leek, halved lengthwise and sliced
Salt
2 cloves garlic, minced
1 tablespoon chopped fresh rosemary
4 cups vegetable stock
2 leaves kale, stemmed and roughly chopped
2 cups drained freshly cooked white beans (cannellini, navy, etc.)
     or one 15-ounce can white beans, rinsed and drained
Pepper
2 teaspoons chopped fresh Italian parsley

In a large pot, heat the oil over medium heat, and add the onion, carrot, leek, and a pinch of salt. Cook for 5 minutes, or until soft. Add the garlic and rosemary, and cook for 3 more minutes. Add the vegetable stock, and simmer for 20 minutes. Add the kale and beans, and simmer for 1 more minute. Season with salt and pepper to taste, stir in the parsley, and serve.

PEANUT BUTTERNUT SQUASH SOUP

||||||||||||||||||||||||||||||||||||||||||||||||||||||||||||||||||||||||||||||||||||||||||||||||||||||

Whaaaaaat??!! I know. Trust me. Oh, and peel the squash with a good potato peeler.

Serves 4 (4 cups)

2 teaspoons extra-virgin olive oil
½ cup plus 1 tablespoon thinly sliced scallions
½ cup diced carrot
Salt
1 pound butternut squash, peeled, seeded, and cut into
    1-inch cubes
3 cups vegetable stock
5 tablespoons Peanut Sauce (see recipe, page 204)
Pepper
¼ cup chopped peanuts, for garnish

In a large pot, heat the oil over medium heat. Add the ½ cup of scallions, the carrot, and a pinch of salt, and sweat until tender, 4 to 5 minutes. Add the squash and the vegetable stock, and bring to a boil. Simmer for 30 minutes, or until the squash is very tender. Use a hand blender or pour the soup into a food processor or blender, and puree until smooth. Stir in the peanut sauce, season with salt and pepper to taste, and garnish with the peanuts and the remaining 1 tablespoon of scallions. Serve.

HARVEST VEGETABLE SOUP

||||||||||||||||||||||||||||||||||||||||||||||||||||||||||||||||||||||||||||||||||||||||||||||||||||||

You can substitute any number of veggies for this soup. Broccoli instead of cauliflower, potatoes instead of zucchini, chard instead of kale, etc. This soup is a great way to cook with the seasons.

Serves 6 (6 cups)

2 teaspoons extra-virgin olive oil
½ cup diced yellow onion
½ cup diced carrot
½ cup diced celery
Salt
2 cloves garlic, minced
2 tablespoons tomato paste
One 15-ounce can diced tomatoes, with juice
4 cups vegetable stock
2 cups drained freshly cooked kidney beans or one 15-ounce
    can kidney beans, rinsed and drained
½ head cauliflower, cut into bite-size pieces
1 small zucchini, cut into bite-size pieces
2 leaves kale, stemmed and roughly chopped
1 tablespoon chopped fresh Italian parsley
Pepper

In a large pot, heat the oil over medium heat and add the onion, carrot, celery, and a healthy pinch of salt. Cook for 3 to 4 minutes, then add the garlic. Continue cooking for 4 to 5 more minutes, until the veggies are tender. Stir in the tomato paste, tomatoes (and juice), and vegetable stock. Simmer for 20 minutes. Add the beans, cauliflower, and zucchini, and simmer for 5 more minutes, or until the cauliflower and zucchini are tender. Turn off the heat, and add the kale. Let sit 5 minutes, until the kale becomes tender. Stir in the parsley, and season with salt and pepper to taste.

SAMBAR

||||||||||||||||||||||||||||||||||||||||||||||||||||||||||||||||||||||||||||||||||||||||||||||||||||||||||||||||||||||||||||||||

Ohhhhh, mama!! This soup makes my mouth water whenever I think about it. There are a few ingredients in this one that you'll only be able to get at an Indian market. If you don't have such a market, you can get the spices on the interwebs. And if you can't find curry leaves or tamarind paste, the world won't explode — you can still make the soup.

Serves 6 (6 cups)

3 teaspoons extra-virgin olive oil
½ cup diced yellow onion
½ cup diced carrot
Salt
1 cup red lentils
4 cups vegetable stock
1 teaspoon black mustard seeds
15 curry leaves
½ pound tomatoes, cut into bite-size pieces
1 tablespoon sambar powder (see WTF, next page)
½ teaspoon tamarind paste
¼ pound green beans, trimmed and cut into bite-size pieces
Pepper

In a large pot, heat 2 teaspoons of the oil over medium heat, and add the onion, carrot, and a healthy pinch of salt. Cook for 4 to 6 minutes, or until the veggies become tender. Add the lentils and 3 cups of the vegetable stock, and simmer for 20 minutes, or until the lentils become very tender.

Meanwhile, heat the remaining 1 teaspoon of oil in another pot or skillet over medium heat. Add the black mustard seeds and curry leaves. When the mustard seeds begin to sizzle and pop, add the tomatoes, a pinch of salt, and the sambar powder, and stir to combine. Cook, stirring occasionally, until the tomatoes become soft, for 8 to 10 minutes.

Now that your lentils are completely cooked, mash them against the side of the pot with the back of a wooden spoon to help thicken the soup. Add the tomato mixture, tamarind paste, and beans, and simmer for 8 more minutes. If the soup is too thick, add as much of the remaining 1 cup of vegetable stock as you want. There is no hard-and-fast rule for thickness, just personal preference. When the green beans are tender, the soup is done. Season with salt and pepper to taste.

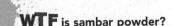

WTF is sambar powder?

Also known as *sambar masala*, sambar powder is a combination of Indian spices, including fenugreek, coriander, and turmeric. It lends great flavor and a little heat to the soup. You can find it at an Indian market or on the interwebs.

CHAPTER 5
Go Fork Yourself!
salads

WE ALL KNOW WHAT SALAD IS. We all know that it's good for us, and we do our best to eat it every day. But many of us do our salads — and ultimately, ourselves — a supreme injustice: we use store-bought dressing. You may already be hip to the fact that we should not be consuming things like calcium disodium ethylenediaminetetraacetic acid, apocarotenal, or Red 40…I mean, c'mon, how can you *eat* a color? I don't really know what any of these are, and they sure don't *sound* like food, but they are passed off as it in popular store-bought salad dressings all the time.

The entree salads in this chapter show you that a salad dressing should contain very few, easily pronounceable ingredients. For instance, a vinaigrette needs only an acid (vinegar or citrus), a fat (any oil, from canola to extra-virgin olive), herbs, spices, and maybe a sweetener (agave or maple syrup, or sugar). To aid in emulsification and to add another layer of flavor, a small amount of Dijon or grain mustard can be added as well. You can even go creamy by adding a little pureed silken tofu or vegan mayo to the mix. The point is: There's a bunch of bad shit out there. You can easily make your own salad dressings at home, in very little time, with very little effort. You also don't have to drop a ton of coin on those organic all-natural dressings in the hippie section of the store, when you could be spending it on much more important things…like wine.

ET TU, TEMPEH?

Quod optimum salad. Google translator solebam interpretari ut vertat. Puto ea fere fecit.

Makes 2 entrees or 4 appetizers

One 8-ounce package tempeh
½ cup balsamic vinegar
½ cup low-sodium tamari or soy sauce (see WTF, page 25)
1 tablespoon Blackened Seasoning (see recipe, page 210)
Extra-virgin olive oil
1 small head romaine lettuce or ½ large head, roughly
   chopped
1 cup Creamy Caeser Dressing (recipe follows)
2 cups Croutons (recipe follows)
2 tablespoons Parmesan Topping (see recipe, page 211)

Cut the tempeh into thin squares. In a zip-top bag, combine the vinegar and tamari, and add the tempeh squares. Gently slosh the tempeh around so it gets coated, squeeze the bag to suck out as much of the excess air as possible, and let marinate in the fridge for 1 to 4 hours. Remove the tempeh squares from the marinade and pat dry. Coat with the blackened seasoning and a little olive oil. Heat a medium skillet over medium-high heat, and cook the oiled and seasoned tempeh for 2 to 4 minutes, or until blackened on one side, then flip and repeat. Then cut the tempeh into bite-size pieces.

Finally, toss the lettuce with the dressing, and top the salad with the tempeh, croutons, and parmesan topping.

CREAMY CAESAR DRESSING

Makes 2 cups

1 cup whole raw cashews
4 ounces soft silken tofu
1½ tablespoons fresh lemon juice
1½ teaspoons extra-virgin olive oil
1 tablespoon nutritional yeast (see WTF, page 27)
1½ teaspoons minced garlic
¼ cup water
1 teaspoon capers, drained
¼ teaspoon seaweed powder (see WTF, page 63)
½ teaspoon Dijon mustard
1 teaspoon vegan Worcestershire sauce (see WTF, page 12)
¼ teaspoon yellow miso
Salt and pepper

To make the dressing, in a small pot, cover the cashews with water and boil for 8 minutes, then drain and set aside. In a food processor, combine the boiled cashews, tofu, lemon juice, oil, nutritional yeast, garlic, water, capers, seaweed powder, mustard, Worcestershire, and miso, and puree until smooth. Season with salt and pepper to taste. Store the dressing in a sealed container in the fridge for up to a week.

CROUTONS

Makes 2 cups

2 cups day-old bread cubes, about 1-inch square
½ cup extra-virgin olive oil
¼ teaspoon salt
Pinch of pepper
1 teaspoon fresh lemon juice

Preheat the oven to 350°F. Coat the bread cubes with olive oil, and toss with the salt, a pinch of pepper, and the lemon juice. Spread out the seasoned bread cubes on a baking sheet, and toast in the oven for 10 to 15 minutes. You can also toast them in a large pan over medium heat, about 4 minutes per side.

THE KARATE CHOP

Ha-YA!

Makes 2 entrees or 4 appetizers

1 cup shelled edamame
½ head romaine lettuce, chopped
1 cup diced Granny Smith apple
1 medium carrot, shredded
1 cup diced cucumber
¼ cup thinly sliced scallions
1 cup shredded red cabbage
Sesame seeds, for garnish
Chopped peanuts, for garnish

DRESSING

2 tablespoons sesame oil
1 teaspoon low-sodium tamari or soy sauce (see WTF, page 25)
2 teaspoons rice vinegar
1 teaspoon agave nectar
Pinch of chili flakes

Bring a small pot of water to a boil, drop in your edamame, and boil for 30 seconds. Drain, cool immediately under cold running water, and let drip-dry in a colander. In a small bowl, whisk together the dressing ingredients until combined. In a large bowl, toss the edamame, lettuce, apple, carrot, cucumber, scallions, and cabbage with the dressing. Garnish with sesame seeds and peanuts.

THE GRILLED COBB

||||||||||||||||||||||||||||||||||||||||||||||||||||||||||||||||||||||||||||||||||||||||||||||||||||

My omnivore friends like to give me a good ribbing at barbecues when I throw
the lettuce on the grill: "Oh, how cute — he even grills salad. Heh, heh, heh."
And then they see the finished product, and they're all like, "Um, can I try that?"
And I'm all like, "No! Get out of my friggin' face carcass-muncher!!" I think I might
need new friends.

Makes 2 entrees or 4 appetizers

1 ear corn, husked
1 head romaine, halved lengthwise, with root intact
1 avocado, halved, pitted, halves scooped out of the peel
    and kept intact
1 Roma tomato, halved lengthwise
Extra-virgin olive oil
Salt and pepper
2 Basic Seitan Cutlets (see recipe, pages 24–25)
Blackened Seasoning (see recipe, page 210)
8 strips Tempeh Bacon (see recipe, page 32), fully prepared
    and chopped

DRESSING

¼ cup vegan mayo (see WTF, page 42)
¼ cup Sour Creaminess (see recipe, page 205) or vegan sour
    cream
1 tablespoon Crazy Shit (see recipe, page 194), or pickle relish
1 tablespoon chopped fresh Italian parsley
1 teaspoon garlic powder
1 teaspoon onion powder
Pinch of paprika
Pinch of celery seed

Water as needed to thin out the dressing
Salt and pepper

Preheat a gas or charcoal grill to medium-high heat. Brush the corn and the cut sides of the romaine, avocado, and tomato with olive oil, and season with salt and pepper. Coat the seitan cutlets with olive oil, and rub with the blackened seasoning.

When the grill is hot, grill the corn until it's slightly brown on all sides, 8 to 10 minutes. Remove the corn from the grill and let cool, then use a knife to remove the kernels from the cob; set aside. Place the romaine, avocado, and tomato on the grill, cut sides down, and grill until charred, about 3 minutes for the tomato, 2 minutes for the avocado, and 1 minute for the lettuce. Then throw on the seitan, and grill until it gets sweet grill marks, 3 to 4 minutes per side.

In a small bowl, whisk together the dressing ingredients, including salt and pepper to taste.

To assemble the salad, cut the root ends from the romaine halves, roughly chop the leaves, and pile them up on two plates. Also roughly chop the tomato and avocado. Cut the seitan into strips. Now go look at a picture of a Cobb salad to see where everything goes, or just get creative and artfully place the corn, avocado, tomato, seitan, and tempeh bacon on top of the lettuce in some way that appeals to you. Drizzle the dressing on top.

THE BEET DOWN

||||||||||||||||||||||||||||||||||||||||||||||||||||||||||||||||||||||||||||||||||||||||||||||||||||||||||||||||||||||||||

Just one note before you make and consume this one: Beware the Red Scare! That's when you go to take a whiz, and scream out in horror, "Holy flying shit! I'm friggin' pissing blood!" and you've forgotten that you ate a bunch of beets earlier.

Makes 2 entrees or 4 appetizers

3 medium red beets with greens
1 teaspoon extra-virgin olive oil
Pinch of salt
Pinch of pepper
¼ cup whole raw cashews
2 cups chopped iceberg lettuce
⅓ cup thinly sliced fennel

DRESSING

2 tablespoons extra-virgin olive oil
¼ cup fresh orange juice
¼ teaspoon white wine vinegar
1 teaspoon chopped fresh tarragon
Salt and pepper to taste

Scan to watch the video.

Preheat the oven to 350°F. Cut the greens off the beets, and wash and coarsely chop them. Wash and dry the beets. Toss the beets with the olive oil and a pinch of salt and a pinch of pepper. Individually wrap the beets in foil, leaving little openings for steam to escape. Roast the beets for 1 hour, or until a fork easily pierces them. Remove the beets from the foil, and when they're cool enough to handle, scrape off their skins with a small spoon. Cut the beets into bite-size cubes.

Heat a dry pan over medium heat, and add your cashews, toasting them until they are a little brown on one side, 1 to 2 minutes, and then toss them to brown on the other side, another 1 to 2 minutes. Just keep an eye on them, since those little bastards burn easily. Remove from the pan to cool. When the cashews are cool enough to handle, roughly chop.

In a small bowl, whisk together the dressing ingredients until combined.

In a large bowl, toss the lettuce, beet greens, and fennel with half of the dressing. Pile the salad in the middle of a serving plate, artfully arrange the beets around the edges, and drizzle with the remaining dressing. Finally, top with the chopped cashews.

CURRY FRIED TOFU SALAD

||||||||||||||||||||||||||||||||||||||||||||||||||||||||||||||||||||||||||||||||||||||||||||||||||||||||||||||||||

Food should appeal to all five senses. And this salad is a perfect example of something that stimulates sight, smell, texture, and taste, and if you listen really closely, it gives you great decorating tips.

Makes 2 entrees or 4 appetizers

One 14-ounce block extra-firm tofu, drained (see Tip, page 35)
1 tablespoon extra-virgin olive oil
2 tablespoons curry powder
3 tablespoons unbleached all-purpose flour (or another flour, like garbanzo, rice, etc.)
Pinch of salt
Pinch of pepper
½ head red leaf lettuce, roughly chopped or torn
½ medium cucumber, thinly sliced
1 scallion, thinly sliced
1 medium beet, grated
1 medium carrot, grated

DRESSING

1 small Thai chili, minced (you can use less depending on how hot the peppers are)
½ teaspoon tamarind paste
1 tablespoon fresh lime juice
½ teaspoon low-sodium tamari or soy sauce (see WTF, page 25)
3 tablespoons extra-virgin olive oil
¼ teaspoon agave nectar

Slice the tofu crosswise into six ⅓-inch-thick rectangles. In a frying pan, heat the olive oil over medium-high heat. Spread the curry powder, flour, and salt and pepper on a shallow plate, stir to combine, and dredge both sides of the tofu slices in the seasoning. When the olive oil is just barely starting to smoke, carefully place the slices in the frying pan. Let them fry on one side for 3 to 4 minutes, until browned. Then flip and brown on the other side, 3 to 4 minutes. In a small bowl, whisk together the dressing ingredients. In a large bowl, combine the lettuce, cucumber, scallion, beet, and carrot, and toss with the dressing. Pile the salad on a plate and place the fried tofu on top in an artful fashion.

THE GIRLFRIEND'S FAVORITE SALAD
THAT SHE CONSTANTLY ASKS ME TO MAKE AND **WON'T SHUT THE HELL UP ABOUT**

This *is* a very good salad, so I don't really blame her.

Makes 2 entrees or 4 appetizers

½ head romaine lettuce, chopped into bite-size pieces
1 cup diced cucumber
1 cup drained freshly cooked or rinsed canned chickpeas
1 cup sliced hearts of palm
½ cup diced celery
2 cups Croutons (see recipe, page 82)

DRESSING

¼ cup sherry vinegar
1 teaspoon Dijon mustard
½ teaspoon agave nectar
½ cup extra-virgin olive oil
Salt and pepper

To make the dressing, in a small bowl, whisk together the vinegar, mustard, and agave nectar. When they are combined, stream the olive oil into the bowl, whisking steadily. Season with salt and pepper to taste.

In a large bowl, combine the lettuce, cucumber, chickpeas, hearts of palm, and celery, and toss with the dressing. Scatter the croutons on top.

SOUTHWEST SLAW

||||||||||||||||||||||||||||||||||||||||||||||||||||||||||||||||||||||||||||||||||||||||||||||||||||||||||||||||

A killer side dish for the Black Bean Burger with Kajillion Island Dressing (see page 197).

Makes 4 side servings

3 cups shredded green cabbage
Salt
2 tablespoons vegan mayo (see WTF, page 42)
Juice of ½ lime
1 teaspoon ground chipotle
1 tablespoon chopped fresh cilantro
2 scallions, thinly sliced
½ cup shredded carrot
½ cup drained freshly cooked or rinsed canned black beans
½ cup fresh or thawed frozen corn kernels
Pepper

In a colander, toss the shredded cabbage with a very generous amount of salt (¼ cup or so) and let it drain in the sink for at least 60 minutes, ideally 90. Rinse the cabbage really well with water to wash away the salt. (I know, this sounds counterintuitive — remove water, then add water — but trust me, it works.) It's very important to taste the cabbage at this point to make sure that it's not salty. If it tastes salty, give

TIP

Ahhh...cabbage bound for slaw: to salt or not to salt? What the hell am I talking about? Well, if you make this recipe without salting your cabbage, after about an hour, you'll have a watery and flavor-diluted slaw on your hands. There's a shitload of water in that there cabbage, and salting it removes that water before it becomes part of your dressing. If you're going to serve this slaw right away in all its fresh and crunchy gloriousness, don't worry about salting it beforehand. However, if it's going to sit in a huge bowl all day at a barbecue, or you plan on keeping leftovers for tomorrow, then definitely salt it. This will keep it crunchier, fresher, and flavorful-er, longer.

it another rinse. Spin-dry the cabbage in a salad spinner or pat dry with a paper towel. Now it's ready to become slaw.

In a small bowl, whisk together the mayo, lime juice, chipotle, and cilantro. In a large bowl, combine the cabbage, scallions, carrot, beans, and corn, and toss with the dressing. Season with salt and pepper to taste.

MARINATED EGGPLANT PASTA SALAD

||||||||||||||||||||||||||||||||||||||||||||||||||||||||||||||||||||||||||||||||||||||||||||||||||||||||||||||

I am by no means an eggplant lover. I can deal with it if it's breaded and deep-fried, or sliced super thin and baked until crispy topping a pizza, but keep it away from me in any other forms…especially that goddamned baba ghanoush, BLAH! This preparation, however, has shot to the top of the list of "Ways in Which I Will Consume Eggplant." The eggplant takes on a crunchy, almost pickle-like texture, and the zingy marinade penetrates its every fiber. You have to make this one the day before you plan to eat it, but it's totally worth the wait.

Serves 4 to 6

10 ounces eggplant, cut into ½-inch-thick slices
   (about 5 slices)
 teaspoons salt, plus more as needed
¼ cup thinly sliced scallions
1 clove garlic, minced
¼ cup red wine vinegar, plus more as needed
½ cup extra-virgin olive oil
¼ teaspoon chili flakes
1 teaspoon finely chopped fresh Italian parsley
½ teaspoon finely chopped fresh thyme
Pepper
8 ounces fusilli pasta
½ cup roughly chopped kalamata olives
½ cup roughly chopped oil-packed sun-dried tomatoes
½ packed cup baby spinach

First you need to salt the eggplant slices, which removes excess water and bitterness and allows the marinade to penetrate thoroughly. In a colander, toss the eggplant slices with 2 teaspoons of salt, coating both sides of each slice, and spread out the slices, so that they are not on top of one another. Let them drain in the colander for 90 minutes. Rinse the eggplant really well with water to wash away the salt, and pat dry with paper towels. Finally, cut the eggplant into ¾-inch cubes.

Place the eggplant, scallions, garlic, vinegar, oil, chili flakes, parsley, thyme, ½ teaspoon of salt, and a pinch of pepper in a zip-top bag. Gently slosh the eggplant around so it gets coated, squeeze the bag to suck out as much of the air as possible, and place in the fridge to marinate for at least 8 hours and up to 12 hours.

When marinating is complete, remove the bag from the fridge. You don't need to let the eggplant get all the way to room temperature, but just let it hang out on the counter to take a bit of the chill off of it. Bring a large pot of salted water to a boil. Cook the fusilli according to the directions on the package. Drain the fusilli and cool it by flushing with cold water. Let it drain until it's as dry as possible. In a large bowl, combine the pasta, olives, sun-dried tomatoes, spinach, and eggplant with its marinade. Toss it all together, and season with salt and pepper to taste and an extra splash of red wine vinegar, if desired.

CHICKPEA PARTY

||||||||||||||||||||||||||||||||||||||||||||||||||||||||||||||||||||||||||||||||||||||||||||||||||||||||||||||||

This is something my grandmother would make. Although she would probably try to drop in some cubes of salami and pepperoni, in which case I would have to body-slam her…again.

Serves 4 to 6

⅓ cup extra-virgin olive oil
2 tablespoons red wine vinegar
Salt and pepper
Two 15-ounce cans chickpeas, drained and rinsed
2 roasted red bell peppers, diced (see Tip below)
½ cup diced red onion
1 tablespoon chopped fresh oregano
2 teaspoons dried basil

In a small bowl, whisk together the oil and vinegar, and season with salt and pepper to taste. In a large bowl, combine the chickpeas, bell peppers, onion, oregano, and basil, and toss with the dressing. Season with more salt and pepper to taste.

TIP
To roast a bell pepper:

Put the whole pepper directly over a stove-top flame (or under the broiler). When it blackens on one side, turn it to blacken on another side. Keep turning until it's black all around. Immediately put the roasted pepper into a paper bag, close the top (or put it into a bowl and cover with plastic wrap), and let it hang out for 10 to 15 minutes to steam. The steaming makes it really easy to remove the skin. Remove and discard the blackened skin by hand, and tear the pepper open to remove the seeds…just be careful because very hot steam will be released from the pepper.

SEARED HEARTS OF PALM SALAD

||||||||||||||||||||||||||||||||||||||||||||||||||||||||||||||||||||||||||||||||||||||||||||||||||||||||||||||||||||||||||||||||||||

This salad totally sucks — if you hate things that are awesome.

Makes 2 entrees or 4 appetizers

2 teaspoons extra-virgin olive oil
4 whole hearts of palm, patted dry and cut into 1-inch-long
  segments
Salt and pepper
¼ cup chopped kalamata olives
1 packed cup arugula
1 packed cup torn butter lettuce
1 medium avocado, diced

DRESSING

2 tablespoons chopped oil-packed sun-dried tomatoes
4 tablespoons sun-dried tomato oil or extra-virgin olive oil
1 tablespoon white balsamic vinegar
2 teaspoons chopped fresh basil
Salt and pepper to taste

In a medium skillet, heat 1 teaspoon of the oil over medium-high heat. In a bowl, toss the hearts of palm with the remaining 1 teaspoon of oil and salt and pepper. Place them cut side down in the pan. If there's no sizzle, wait until the oil is hot; otherwise, they will not sear. When golden on one side, flip and repeat. In a food processor or blender, puree the dressing ingredients. In a large bowl, toss the olives, arugula, lettuce, and avocado with the dressing. Arrange on a serving plate. Then cut the hearts of palm in half crosswise, so you can display the seared sides, and artfully place them around the outside of the plate.

CHAPTER 6
Handheld
sandwiches

||||||||||||||||||||||||||||||||||||||||||||||||||||||||||||||||||||||||||||||||||||||||||||||||||||||||||||||||||||||||||

IF YOU'RE A BUSY EXECUTIVE always on the go, just like me, you don't always have time to sit down and have a proper meal. Things move pretty fast these days, and we need to be mobile. Mobile phones, mobile computers…mobile food. Whether you're crawling at 8 mph or cruising at 80 mph, the following items are all designed to be eaten with one hand on the wheel and one hand on your food. Some of them may require two hands to eat, so just do the slide-down-the-seat-steer-with-your-knee thing. They're so delicious, it's worth the risk.

THE SEITAN WORSHIPPER

||||||||||||||||||||||||||||||||||||||||||||||||||||||||||||||||||||||||||||||||||||||||||||||||||||||||||||||||||||||||||

A cross between a Philly cheesesteak and a patty melt, this devilishly delicious sandwich will have you questioning your religion. Wow! That sounded like something that would be written in a cookbook. I promise I won't let it happen again.

Makes 2 sandwiches

7 teaspoons vegan margarine
½ cup sliced red onion
Salt
8 ounces Basic Seitan Slices (see recipe, pages 24–25), about 16 slices
8 tablespoons Smoked Cheddar Sauce (see recipe, page 215)
4 slices sourdough bread

In a medium skillet, melt 1 teaspoon of the margarine over medium-high heat. Add the onion and a pinch of salt. Cook, without stirring, until the onion begins to brown, about 3 to 5 minutes, then flip and cook for 3 to 4 more minutes, until softened. Push the onion to the side of the pan, and add the seitan slices. Cook for 1 to 2 minutes, just enough to warm up and slightly brown the seitan, and then toss with the onion. Cook for 1 more minute, then turn off the heat.

Spread 1 teaspoon of margarine on one side of each bread slice, flip the bread slices over, and spread 2 tablespoons of the smoked cheddar sauce on the other side of each. Place the seitan-onion mixture on top of the cheeze sauce on two of the bread slices, and then place the other two slices of bread, cheeze sauce side down, on top.

In another medium skillet, heat 2 teaspoons of margarine over medium heat, for guaranteed lubrication. Carefully place the sandwiches in the pan. Cook for 5 to 7 minutes, or until golden, then flip and brown the other side, 5 to 7 more minutes.

THE S.I.L.F.

Some sandwiches you just want to be friends with, and others, well...

Makes 2 sandwiches

2 focaccia rolls, sliced in half
8 tablespoons hummus (see Golden Beet Hummus recipe,
    page 179, or use store-bought)
½ medium cucumber, thinly sliced
1 roasted poblano pepper, halved (see Tip, page 96)
1 medium heirloom tomato, cut into ¼-inch-thick slices
1 tablespoon fresh basil chiffonade (see WTF below)
1 small handful arugula

Lightly toast the focaccia, and spread 2 tablespoons of hummus on each toasted focaccia half. Top two of the focaccia halves with the cucumber, poblano, tomato, basil, and arugula. Then place the other two focaccia halves, hummus side down, on top.

WTF is basil chiffonade?
To get these fancy-schmancy ribbons of deliciousness,
stack several leaves on top of one another,
roll them up like a cigar, and thinly slice them.

THE QUOTE-UNQUOTE TUNA MELT

||||||||||||||||||||||||||||||||||||||||||||||||||||||||||||||||||||||||||||||||||||||||||||||||||||||||||||||||||||||||||||||||||

A late-night, post-bar, greasy-diner classic. If I had a nickel for every time I drunkenly ordered a tuna melt with a side of Denver omelette at 2:30 in the morning, I'd have *sooo* many nickels.

Makes 2 sandwiches

One 15-ounce can chickpeas, drained and rinsed
1 stalk celery, diced
1 tablespoon minced red onion
1 tablespoon capers, drained and chopped
½ teaspoon seaweed powder (see WTF, page 63)
1 teaspoon Dijon mustard
1 tablespoon fresh lemon juice
3 tablespoons vegan mayo (see WTF, page 42)
1 tablespoon Crazy Shit (see recipe, page 194) or sweet
    pickle relish
Salt and pepper
2 tablespoons vegan margarine
4 slices bread of your choice
4 slices vegan cheeze or 2 tablespoons Not-zzarella Sauce
    (see recipe, page 214)

In a medium bowl, mash the chickpeas with a fork, potato masher, or your very clean hands, until about 70 percent of the beans are mashed. Add the celery and red onion, and set aside.

In a separate bowl, whisk together the capers, seaweed powder, mustard, lemon juice, mayo, and crazy shit or relish. Add the mayo mixture to the chickpea bowl, and mix everything together. Season with salt and pepper to taste.

Heat a skillet over medium heat. Spread ½ tablespoon of margarine on one side of each bread slice and flip the bread slices over. Put 2 slices of cheeze or 1 tablespoon of not-zzarella sauce on the other side of 2 of the bread slices. Top the 2 cheeze-covered bread slices with the chickpea mixture and the remaining 2 slices of bread, margarine side up. Place the sandwiches in the hot skillet. Cook for 5 to 7 minutes per side, or until each side is golden.

THE PORTLY FELLOW

If this sandwich were a person, he would be a round, top hat–wearing gentleman in an old-timey suit with a pocket watch, monocle, and cane. And despite his size, he would eat sandwiches in a dainty fashion. That makes me smile.

Makes 2 sandwiches

2 portobello mushrooms, stemmed and wiped clean
2½ teaspoons extra-virgin olive oil
2 teaspoons balsamic vinegar
Salt and pepper
½ cup sliced red onion
2 ciabatta rolls, halved and toasted
½ cup Sun-Dried Tomato and White Bean Spread (recipe follows)
1 roasted red bell pepper, halved (see Tip, page 96)
1 small handful baby arugula
1 medium tomato, sliced

Preheat the oven to 350°F. Coat the mushrooms with 2 teaspoons of the oil, the vinegar, and a pinch of salt and a pinch of pepper. Place the mushrooms in the smallest roasting vessel that will hold them. The smaller the vessel, the more of the delicious mushroom juice that will collect during cooking, so make sure the vessel has sides. You can make one out of foil if need be. On a baking sheet, toss the onion slices with the remaining ½ teaspoon of oil, a pinch of salt, and a pinch of pepper, and spread them out. Roast both the shrooms and the onion for 15 to 20 minutes, or until soft. Remove the mushrooms and onion from the oven, and let cool, making sure to reserve any mushroom juices that have accumulated. Cut the shrooms thinly on the diagonal, so that you create wide, flat slices.

Scan to watch the video.

Now you're ready to assemble! Remember those shroom juices you were trying to preserve? Drizzle them on the bottom half of each of the ciabatta rolls (if there's not enough, don't get your butt-hole all a-pucker — just drizzle some additional oil and vinegar on the ciabatta to compensate), and smear the top halves with the bean spread.

Assemble each of the sandwiches from the bottom up in the following order: bottom ciabatta half, sliced shrooms, roasted pepper, roasted onion, arugula, tomato, and bean-smeared ciabatta half.

SUN-DRIED TOMATO AND WHITE BEAN SPREAD

This is also a great dip for chips or veggies. Store extra in a sealed container in the fridge for up to a week.

Makes about 2 cups

2 cups drained freshly cooked cannellini beans or one
    15-ounce can cannellini beans, rinsed and drained
4 medium basil leaves
2 tablespoons chopped sun-dried tomatoes
1 tablespoon sun-dried tomato oil or extra-virgin olive oil
¼ cup water
1 clove garlic
Salt and pepper

In a food processor or blender, puree the beans, basil, sun-dried tomatoes, oil, water, and garlic until smooth. Season with salt and pepper to taste.

THE FAT ASS
|||||||||||||||||||||||||||||||||||||||||||||||||||||||||||||||||||||||||||||||||||||||||||||||||||||||||||||||||

This is the one you whip out for the big party. The Super Bowl, the Oscars, the Grey Cup (I'm winking at you, Canada), etc. Get a long roll and quadruple this recipe, and jaws will hit the floor.

Makes 2 sandwiches

Two 6-inch hoagie rolls
½ cup Kajillion Island Dressing (see recipe, page 197)
6 strips Tempeh Bacon (see recipe, page 32)
8 ounces Basic Seitan Slices (see recipe, pages 24–25), about
    16 slices
½ avocado, thinly sliced
½ cup shredded green cabbage
1 medium tomato, thinly sliced

Cut the rolls open lengthwise, leaving a "bread hinge," and smear each roll with ¼ cup kajillion island dressing. Assemble the sandwiches from the bottom up in the following order: 3 strips of bacon, 4 ounces of seitan slices, half of the avocado slices, ¼ cup of cabbage, and half of the tomato slices.

BOURBON TEMPEH SLIDERS

If you're only making one batch of these sliders, I recommend that you eat them alone. If someone walks in on you, you'd best get into an elbowy defensive position and prepare for battle.

Makes 6 sliders

4 teaspoons extra-virgin olive oil
One 8-ounce package tempeh, cut into six 2-inch-by-2-inch-by-¼-inch squares
1 red onion, thinly sliced
½ cup bourbon
1 teaspoon brown sugar
1 cup vegetable stock
2 teaspoons arrowroot dissolved in 1 teaspoon water (see WTF, page 69)
Salt and pepper
3 tablespoons Smoked Cheddar Sauce (optional), warmed
6 mini buns (about 2 inches wide), halved
¼ packed cup baby spinach
1 Roma tomato, cut into 6 slices

In a pan, heat 2 teaspoons of the oil over medium-high heat. Add the tempeh to the pan, and fry for 2 to 3 minutes, or until browned on one side, then flip and brown the other side, 2 to 3 minutes. Remove the tempeh from the pan, and set aside. Add the onion to the same pan and saute for 4 to 5 minutes, or until slightly browned and soft. So as to not set yourself on fire, turn off the flame, and add the bourbon to the pan. Now let the bourbon simmer over medium heat for 1 minute, or until reduced by half.

Stir in the brown sugar, and simmer until it dissolves, about 1 minute. Add the vegetable stock, and simmer for 2 to 3 more minutes. Stir in the arrowroot slurry, continuing to simmer for about 1 more minute. When the sauce begins to thicken, add the tempeh to the pan and coat it with the sauce. Cook for 1 to 2 more minutes, or until the sauce reduces to a glaze. Season with salt and pepper to taste.

Time for assembly. If using the smoked cheddar sauce, spread it on the inside of the buns. Assemble the sandwiches from the bottom up in the following order: 1 bun half, 1 piece of tempeh, a little of the bourbon sauce and onions, a few spinach leaves, 1 tomato slice, a pinch of salt, and the other bun half.

THE BEANY TAHINI BURGER

||||||||||||||||||||||||||||||||||||||||||||||||||||||||||||||||||||||||||||||||||||||||||||||||||||||||||||

Frickin' chickpeas, man. They just do everything, don't they? They're the best. Chickpeas.

Makes 4 burgers

One 15-ounce can chickpeas, drained and rinsed
½ cup cooked couscous
1 tablespoon tahini
1 clove garlic, grated
1 tablespoon chopped fresh oregano
2 tablespoons chopped kalamata olives
1½ teaspoons salt
¼ teaspoon pepper
½ roasted red bell pepper, diced (see Tip, page 96)
2 tablespoons extra-virgin olive oil
4 buns of your choosing, halved
2 tablespoons Dreamy Tahini Dressing (see recipe, page 198)
½ medium cucumber, thinly sliced
2 cups shredded romaine lettuce
1 beefsteak tomato, thinly sliced
½ red onion, thinly sliced

To make the burger patty, in a large bowl, combine the chickpeas, couscous, tahini, garlic, oregano, olives, salt, and pepper. With a fork, potato masher, or your very clean hands, mash all of it together until 90 percent of the chickpeas are mashed. Now that you have this pasty mass, gently fold in the roasted pepper (as it would have been destroyed during the initial mixing). Divide the chickpea mixture into four portions and form into ¼-inch-thick patties.

In a large skillet, heat the oil over medium-high heat. Add your burger patties to the pan, and cook them for 3 to 4 minutes per side, or until golden brown. Slather each bun half with dreamy tahini dressing, and assemble the burgers from the bottom up in the following order: 1 bun half, cucumber, chickpea patty, lettuce, tomato, onion, and the other bun half.

BLACK BEAN BURGER WITH KAJILLION ISLAND DRESSING

||||||||||||||||||||||||||||||||||||||||||||||||||||||||||||||||||||||||||||||||||||||||||||||||||||||||

You know those seemingly useless tortilla crumbs at the bottom of the bag? Yeah, you do! I know you've come home ravenous from the bar to find half a jar of salsa but only tiny chips with which to scoop it. And since all of your bowls are dirty, you have to go right into the jar, getting more salsa on the back of your hand than on that puny chip. Well, I've developed a way to put those chips to good use in this burger. So just be sure to always keep a full bag of tortillas on hand for all of your salsa-consuming needs, and when you get to the bottom, make these burgers. BTW, the Southwest Slaw (see recipe, page 92) is a great side for this burger.

Makes 4 burgers

2 cups drained freshly cooked black beans or one
    15-ounce can black beans, rinsed and drained
2 tablespoons diced red bell pepper
1 cup cooked brown rice, cooled
¼ cup thinly sliced scallions
1 teaspoon adobo sauce
½ cup ground tortilla chips (ground in a food processor or
    blender)
1 teaspoon ground cumin
¾ teaspoon salt
Pepper
¼ cup fresh or thawed frozen corn kernels
2 tablespoons extra-virgin olive oil, for frying
4 whole-wheat buns, halved
1 cup Kajillion Island Dressing (see recipe, page 197)
4 thick slices beefsteak tomato
2 cups shredded romaine lettuce

In a large bowl, combine the beans, bell pepper, rice, scallions, adobo sauce, chips, cumin, salt, and a pinch of pepper. With a fork, potato masher, or your very clean hands, mash everything together, until about 90 percent of the beans are mashed. Now that you have this pasty mass, gently fold in the corn kernels (as they would have been destroyed during the initial mixing). Divide the bean mixture into four portions and form into ¼-inch-thick patties.

In a large skillet, heat the oil over medium-high heat. Add your burger patties to the pan, and cook them for 3 to 4 minutes per side, or until golden brown. If you're using your time wisely, you'll be toasting your buns while the burgers are cooking. Slather each toasted bun half with kajillion island dressing, and assemble the burgers from the bottom up in the following order: 1 bun half, 1 black bean patty, 1 tomato slice, ½ cup of lettuce, and the other bun half.

CHAPTER 7
The Dinner Bell
entrees

IF I WERE WRITING THIS BOOK WHEN I WAS SIXTEEN YEARS OLD, the "Pizza!" chapter would have been titled "Entrees," and the entree chapter would have been titled "The Stuff That Other People, Besides Me, Eat at Dinnertime Instead of Pizza." (Sorry, Mom, that was the last one.) The hearty meals in this chapter are as diverse as they are delicious, and they are sure to fully satisfy vegans and omnivores alike. I *would* say, "It's time to ring the dinner bell," but while other people were made aware of dinnertime by the sound of a ringing dinner bell, I was made aware of dinnertime by the sound of a ringing doorbell. (Okay, *that* was the last one, Mom. Promise.)

SPAGHETTI AND BALLS

|||||||||||||||||||||||||||||||||||||||||||||||||||||||||||||||||||||||||||||||||||||||||||||||||||||||||||||||||

I know I probably don't need to actually write this one down for you, but I just wanted to say "balls" again. Balls.

Serves 4

8 ounces spaghetti

1½ cups Tomato Killer (see recipe, page 200), warmed

12 My Balls (see recipe, page 26), fully prepared and kept warm in a low oven

2 tablespoons Parmesan Topping (see recipe, page 211), for garnish

2 tablespoons chopped fresh Italian parsley, for garnish

Cook the spaghetti according to the directions on the package, and drain. In a large bowl, toss the cooked pasta with ¾ cup of the tomato killer. In a separate bowl, gently toss my balls with the remaining ¾ cup of the tomato killer. Pile your pasta on a plate and top it with your saucy balls — or my saucy balls, as it were — and garnish with the parmesan and parsley.

LASAGNA FAUXLOGNESE

||||||||||||||||||||||||||||||||||||||||||||||||||||||||||||||||||||||||||||||||||||||||||||||||||||||||

This is probably the best thing I make. Wait. Strike that. The *best* thing I make is sweet love to the Girlfriend. This is the *second* best thing I make...although she probably thinks it's the first.

Serves 6

1 teaspoon extra-virgin olive oil
One 9-ounce box no-boil lasagna noodles
2 cups Cashew Ricotta (see recipe, page 213)
3 cups Fauxlognese Sauce (see recipe, page 202)
1 tablespoon Parmesan Topping (see recipe, page 211)
½ cup Not-zzarella Sauce (see recipe, page 214) or other
    vegan cheese
1 tablespoon chopped fresh Italian parsley, for garnish

Preheat the oven to 350°F. Lube up an 8-by-6-by-2-inch casserole dish with the olive oil, and layer the ingredients in the following order: 1 layer of noodles, 1 cup of ricotta, 1 cup fauxlognese, 1 layer of noodles, the remaining 1 cup of ricotta, 1 cup of fauxlognese, 1 layer of noodles, the remaining 1 cup of fauxlognese.

Cover the dish with foil and bake it for 40 minutes, or until the top layer of noodles is easily pierced with a fork. Remove the foil and sprinkle the top with the parmesan topping. Then drizzle the not-zzarella sauce in a very artful fashion on top of that. (Using a squeeze bottle and doing a zigzag formation makes for a cool presentation.) Put the lasagna back in the oven for 5 more minutes, to heat the cheeze topping, then remove it from the oven and let it rest for 8 to 10 minutes before serving. Garnish with parsley.

STUFFED SHELLS PUTTANESCA

||||||||||||||||||||||||||||||||||||||||||||||||||||||||||||||||||||||||||||||||||||||||||||||||||||||||||||||||||

This dish makes me think of family. And whores.

Serves 4

4 teaspoons extra-virgin olive oil, plus more for coating the
    casserole dish
½ cup diced yellow onion
4 cloves garlic, sliced
Pinch of chili flakes
4 cups chopped tomatoes, with juice (ideally fresh, but canned
    is fine)
½ teaspoon vegan Worcestershire sauce (see WTF, page 12)
¼ cup chopped pitted green olives
¼ cup chopped pitted black or kalamata olives
2 teaspoons capers, drained and chopped
4 teaspoons fresh basil chiffonade (see WTF, page 103)
Salt and pepper
2 packed cups stemmed and coarsely chopped kale leaves
12 jumbo pasta shells
1½ cups Cashew Ricotta (see recipe, page 213)
Not-zzarella Sauce (see recipe, page 214) or other vegan
    cheese
Parmesan Topping (see recipe, page 211)

Preheat the oven to 350°F. Bring a large pot of water to a boil for
the pasta. Meanwhile, in a saucepan, heat 2 teaspoons of oil over
medium heat. Add the onion and garlic, and cook gently for 4 to
5 minutes, until the onion softens and the edges of the garlic start
to brown. Add the chili flakes and tomatoes, with their juice. Simmer for 6 minutes, then add the Worcestershire, olives, capers, and

2 teaspoons of basil. Toss together, simmer for 4 more minutes, then season with salt and pepper to taste.

Once the pasta water is boiling and before you cook your shells, drop the kale into the water to cook for 30 seconds. Remove the kale with a slotted spoon and cool it immediately under cold running water. Once the kale has cooled, squeeze as much water from it as you can, chop into smaller pieces, and set aside.

Cook the pasta shells until al dente, about 2 minutes less than the directions on the package recommend. Drain, and cool them immediately under cold running water. Toss the shells with the remaining 2 teaspoons of oil to prevent them from drying out and sticking together, and place them on a baking sheet or plate. Stir the kale into the cashew ricotta, then, using a spoon, stuff 2 tablespoons of the ricotta-kale mixture into each shell.

Lube up a casserole dish with some oil, and spread a thin layer of the tomato sauce on the bottom. Arrange the stuffed shells on top in neat rows, open side up. Pour the remaining sauce over the shells, cover with foil, and bake for 30 to 35 minutes, until the shells are easily pierced with a fork. Turn off the oven and set the broiler on high. Spread the not-zzarella evenly across the top, sprinkle on the parmesan topping, and place the dish under the broiler for 2 to 3 minutes, until the topping is slightly browned. Garnish with the remaining 2 teaspoons of basil. Serve.

OYSTER MUSHROOM RISOTTO

||||||||||||||||||||||||||||||||||||||||||||||||||||||||||||||||||||||||||||||||||||||||||||||||||||||||||||||||||||||||||||||

Make this one, ladies, and I *guarantee* that you will get into your man's pants. I know it's tough for you girls to get laid sometimes, and I'm here to help.

Serves 4

8 cups vegetable stock
Two 2-by-4-inch pieces wakame, (see WTF, next page)
1 tablespoon extra-virgin olive oil
1 cup minced shallot
½ cup diced celery
Salt
4 tablespoons vegan margarine
1 pound oyster mushrooms, roughly chopped
Freshly ground pepper
¼ cup fresh lemon juice
1½ cups arborio rice
2 cups prosecco
2 tablespoons chopped fresh Italian parsley
¼ cup thinly sliced scallions (tops only), for garnish

In a saucepan, bring the vegetable stock and wakame to a simmer. In a medium skillet, heat the oil over medium heat, and add the shallot, celery, and a pinch of salt. Cook for 5 to 7 minutes, until the shallot is soft and translucent. While your shallot and celery are cooking, heat another medium skillet over medium-high heat and melt the margarine. When it's melted, drop in the mushrooms. Toss them in the margarine, and let them cook on one side until they begin to brown, about 5 minutes. Add a pinch of salt, some pepper, and the lemon juice, and give it all a toss. Continue cooking the mushrooms, tossing occasionally, for 6 to 8 more minutes, until they are completely tender. Set aside.

When the shallots in the first skillet are translucent, stir in the rice. Cook, stirring frequently, until the edges of the rice become slightly translucent, 3 to 4 minutes, then add the prosecco. With a wooden spoon, stir the rice in a clockwise motion (unless you're left-handed, or in the Southern Hemisphere...actually, it doesn't really matter, just pick whichever direction feels most natural and stick with it). When the pan is almost completely dry, add ½ cup of the heated vegetable stock (omitting the wakame) and continue stirring. When the pan is almost dry again, add another ½ cup of the stock and continue stirring. Repeat this process until the rice is soft and creamy but not completely mushy...or as we fancy-schmancy chefs like to say, "al dente." You may not need all the vegetable stock. The total cooking time for the rice will be about 20 minutes.

When the rice is done cooking, turn off the heat and stir in the mushrooms and parsley. Season with salt and pepper to taste, pile high on a serving plate, and garnish with the scallions.

WTF is wakame?

In addition to being a really fun word to say, wakame (pronounced WAH-kuh-may) is an edible seaweed that lends a subtly-sweet-yet-salty-from-the-sea flavor to soups, sauces, and broths. Find it in a Japanese market, in the Asian section of your grocery store, or on the interwebs.

GRILLED SEITAN CAPONATA WITH LEMON PILAF

||||||||||||||||||||||||||||||||||||||||||||||||||||||||||||||||||||||||||||||||||||||||||||||||||||||||||

This dish, I admit, is quite a production, but it is impressive. If you want to save time, you can make the caponata and marinate the seitan the day before. Then you can just reheat the caponata and grill the seitan right before serving. And if you *really* don't feel like doing the whole caponata thing, a hearty store-bought marinara sauce will also work.

Serves 4

1 cup extra-virgin olive oil
1 cup fresh lemon juice
4 cloves garlic, minced
1 tablespoon chopped fresh oregano
2 teaspoons chopped fresh rosemary
8 Basic Seitan Cutlets (see recipe, pages 24–25)
Salt and pepper
4 cups Lemon Pilaf (recipe follows)
2 cups Caponata (recipe follows)
2 tablespoons fresh basil chiffonade (see WTF, page 103),
    for garnish
2 tablespoons chopped fresh Italian parsley, for garnish

Combine the oil, lemon juice, garlic, oregano, and rosemary in a large zip-top bag. Add the seitan cutlets, gently slosh them around so they get coated, squeeze the bag to suck out as much of the air as possible, and then seal it. Let the seitan marinate in the fridge for 1 to 4 hours.

Heat a grill, grill pan, or skillet to high. Remove the cutlets from the bag, shake off the excess marinade, and season with salt and pepper. Place the cutlets on the grill or skillet, and sear each side for 2 to 3 minutes, until you have grill marks or brownage.

Divide the pilaf onto 4 plates, lean two seitan cutlets against each pile of pilaf, and spoon ½ cup of the caponata on top of each plate. Garnish with basil and parsley.

LEMON PILAF

Makes 4 cups

1 tablespoon vegan margarine
1 cup diced yellow onion
1 cup diced celery
4 cloves garlic, chopped
Salt
1 teaspoon chopped fresh thyme
2 cups brown rice
4½ cups vegetable stock, plus more if needed
1 tablespoon fresh lemon juice
Zest of 2 medium lemons
2 teaspoons chopped fresh Italian parsley
½ cup slivered almonds
Pepper

In a pot, melt the margarine over medium heat. Add the onion, celery, garlic, and a pinch of salt, and cook for 4 minutes. Add the thyme, and cook for 3 more minutes. Add the rice to the pot, stir to coat it with the margarine and veggies, and cook for 3 to 4 minutes, until the rice starts to become translucent. Add the vegetable stock and cover the pot. When it boils, reduce to a simmer and cook for 35 to 40 minutes, or until the liquid is absorbed and the rice is fully cooked. If the rice is not fully cooked, add more stock and continue cooking. Finally, transfer the rice to a bowl, and stir in the lemon juice, zest, parsley, and almonds. Season with salt and pepper to taste.

CAPONATA

Makes 4 cups

6 large ½-inch-thick rounds peeled eggplant
Salt
2 tablespoons extra-virgin olive oil
4 cloves garlic, sliced
4 medium shallots, sliced
½ pound cremini mushrooms, halved
2 cups diced zucchini
1 cup diced red bell pepper
¼ teaspoon chili flakes
1 tablespoon chopped fresh oregano
2 cups Tomato Killer (see recipe, page 200)
½ cup chopped pitted kalamata olives
2 tablespoons capers, drained
2 cups drained freshly cooked cannellini beans or one
    15-ounce can cannellini beans, rinsed and drained
1 tablespoon fresh basil chiffonade (see WTF, page 103)
Pepper

Before you do anything else you've got to salt your eggplant. This removes excess water and bitterness. Place your eggplant rounds in a colander in the sink, and dust both sides generously with salt. Let them sit like this for 90 minutes, then rinse and pat dry, and dice them.

In a large pan, heat the oil over medium-high heat. Add the garlic, shallots, and a pinch of salt. When the garlic slices become slightly brown around the edges, add the mushrooms, zucchini, bell pepper, eggplant, chili flakes, oregano, and a pinch of salt, and stir. Cook for 6 minutes, or until the veggies become soft, then stir in the tomato killer, olives, and capers. Simmer for 8 minutes. Finally, stir in the beans and basil, and season with salt and pepper to taste.

TIP

This will yield more caponata than you'll need! It will be used again in the pizza chapter, so store it in a sealed container in the fridge for up to 5 days.

COLONEL SCHMOLONEL'S FRIED SEITAN WITH MASHED TATERS, GRAVY, AND GREENS

||||||||||||||||||||||||||||||||||||||||||||||||||||||||||||||||||||||||||||||||||||||||||||||||||||||||||

White suit–wearin', stupid facial hair–havin', false military rank–assumin' poultry peddlers, better head for the hills — your days are numbered.

Serves 4

1 cup unsweetened nondairy milk

½ teaspoon Crazy Shit Vinegar (see recipe, page 194) or apple cider vinegar

8 Basic Seitan Cutlets (see recipe, pages 24–25)

2 cups unbleached all-purpose flour

¼ cup nutritional yeast (see WTF, page 27)

4 teaspoons garlic powder

4 teaspoons onion powder

2 teaspoons paprika

Pinch of cayenne

¼ teaspoon dried thyme

¼ teaspoon dried sage

¼ teaspoon dried rosemary

1 teaspoon mustard powder

1 teaspoon celery seed

1 teaspoon salt, plus more as needed

¼ teaspoon pepper, plus more as needed

½ cup extra-virgin olive oil, for frying

1 cup White Gravy (recipe follows)

Mashed Taters (recipe follows)

Greens (recipe follows)

In a baking dish or shallow bowl, whisk together the nondairy milk and vinegar, and submerge the seitan cutlets in the mixture. Let marinate for 30 minutes at room temperature. On a plate or in a baking dish, combine the flour, nutritional yeast, garlic powder, onion powder, paprika, cayenne, thyme, sage, rosemary, mustard, celery seed, salt, and pepper.

In a large skillet, heat the oil over medium-high heat. We're looking for a shallow fry here, so the oil should be about ¼ inch deep. To test the oil for the proper heat level, drop a tiny bit of flour into it — if it sizzles and bubbles immediately, it's ready.

Remove the cutlets from the wet mixture, shake off the excess liquid, and coat them completely with the flour-and-spice mixture. Shake off the excess dry mix, and dip the cutlets back into the wet mixture. Then dredge the cutlets one more time in the dry mixture, and gently place each one in the heated oil.

Fry for 3 to 4 minutes, or until brown on one side, then flip. Fry for 3 to 4 more minutes. When the cutlets are golden brown, remove them from the pan and place them on a paper towel. Season each with a pinch of salt and pepper. Place two cutlets on each plate, top with white gravy, and serve with mashed taters and greens.

WHITE GRAVY

Makes 1 cup

1 tablespoon vegan margarine
1 cup unsweetened nondairy milk
1 tablespoon unbleached all-purpose flour
1 teaspoon nutritional yeast (see WTF, page 27)
¼ teaspoon salt
Pepper

In a small saucepan, melt the margarine over medium heat. In a separate pot, gently heat the milk. Stir the flour into the pan with the margarine and cook for 3 to 4 minutes, until it forms a blond-colored paste. This is called a roux, which is a froufrou Frenchie term for "thing that will thicken your sauce." Add the heated milk to the roux and whisk together until smooth. Gently bring to a simmer, at which point it will slightly bubble and begin to thicken. After 2 to 3 minutes of simmering, the sauce will be thick enough to coat the back of a spoon. Add the nutritional yeast and salt, and whisk until smooth. Finally, season with pepper to taste.

MASHED TATERS

Serves 4

2 pounds Yukon Gold potatoes, peeled and quartered
¾ cup unsweetened nondairy milk
¼ cup vegan margarine, melted
Salt and pepper

In a large pot, cover the potatoes with cold water. Turn the heat to high, and boil until the potatoes are very soft, about 20 minutes. Drain the potatoes in a colander, shake them dry, and return them to the hot pot. Place the pot back on the stove over low heat for 1 minute (this will help further dry out the potatoes).

TIP

I *must* stress, if you really want to make the best potato possible, then you'll get a potato ricer or a food mill. They'll be so fluffy that you won't want to eat them — you'll want to sleep on them (not recommended). Trust me on this one.

In a small saucepan, heat the nondairy milk on low until it's warm to the touch. While the potatoes are still hot, pass them through your ricer or food mill into a bowl, or, if you disobeyed my earlier command, mash them with a potato masher. But I must warn you, overmashing makes a gummy, glutinous potato, so be careful. With a rubber spatula, stir in the margarine. Stir in half of the milk, and then slowly add more until the potatoes reach the desired consistency. Season with salt and pepper to taste.

GREENS

Serves 4

2 teaspoons extra-virgin olive oil
3 cloves garlic, sliced
Pinch of chili flakes
8 packed cups stemmed and roughly chopped hearty greens
    (kale, collard, chard, etc.)
Salt and pepper

In a large skillet, heat the oil over medium-high heat. Add the garlic and chili flakes, and saute until the garlic begins to brown around the edges. Add the greens and a pinch of salt, and toss. Cook for 4 to 6 minutes, until wilted. Season with salt and pepper to taste.

BARBECUE RIBZ WITH SMOKY ELBOWS AND CHEEZE

||||||||||||||||||||||||||||||||||||||||||||||||||||||||||||||||||||||||||||||||||||

If you don't want to o.d. on wheat gluten, the tofu option (see Variation, next page) is just as killer as the seitan version. Try both.

Serves 4

2 recipes Basic Seitan dough, uncooked (see recipe, page 24)
1 cup vegetable stock
1 cup Crazy Shit Vinegar (see recipe, page 194)
½ cup extra-virgin olive oil, plus more for coating pan
¼ teaspoon liquid smoke (see WTF, page 32)
¼ cup low-sodium tamari or soy sauce (see WTF, page 25)
1 tablespoon plus 1 teaspoon Blackened Seasoning (see recipe, page 210)
2 cups Barbecrazyshit Sauce (see recipe, page 196)
Smoky Elbows and Cheeze (recipe follows)

TIP

Freeze that tofu! The act of completely freezing and then thawing the tofu gives it a very different texture that is difficult to explain with English words. In Klingon, I believe it's pronounced "Ker-macH."* Simply drain your tofu well (see Tip, page 35), wrap it in plastic, and freeze it solid. Then take it out and let it thaw completely. You can then press down on it a little, and more water will come out. This makes the tofu very open to marinades and gives it a firmer texture. I recommend trying it with lots of different recipes as well.

* Not actual Klingon.

Preheat the oven to 350°F. Coat two 6-by-8-inch casserole dishes with some olive oil, and split the seitan and press half into a flat rectangle (about ¼ inch thick) in each dish. Just barely cover the seitan with vegetable stock, and place something heavy on top of it, like another casserole dish. Bake the seitan for 1 hour. Discard the liquid, and cut the seitan into rib-like strips.

Scan to watch the video.

In a small bowl, combine the vinegar, the ½ cup of oil, the liquid smoke, tamari, and blackened seasoning. Pour the mixture into a zip-top bag, add the seitan ribz, gently slosh them around so they get coated, squeeze the bag to suck out as much of the air as possible, and place them in the fridge to marinate for 1 to 4 hours.

Shake off the excess marinade and slather the seitan with a nice layer of barbecrazyshit sauce. Bake the seitan on a baking sheet for 15 minutes, remove it from the oven and brush on a second layer of sauce, and bake for 5 more minutes. Serve with smoky elbows and cheeze.

VARIATION: Barbecue Tofu with Smoky Elbows and Cheeze

Substitute two 14-ounce blocks of extra-firm tofu for the seitan. Drain the tofu, freeze it, and let it thaw completely (see Tip above), then cut it into rectangular strip things. You will not need the veggie stock. Marinate and sauce the tofu as instructed for the seitan. Bake it for 25 minutes, remove it from the oven and brush on a second layer of sauce, and bake for another 20 minutes.

SMOKY ELBOWS AND CHEEZE

Serves 4 to 6

⅓ pound mini elbow pasta
2⅓ cups Smoked Cheddar Sauce (see recipe, page 215)
2 cups panko bread crumbs (see WTF, next page)
2 tablespoons extra-virgin olive oil, plus more for coating pan
¼ teaspoon salt, if needed
Pepper, if needed

Preheat the oven to 350°F. Cook the pasta until al dente, about 2 minutes less than the directions on the package recommend. Drain, and toss with the cheeze sauce. Lube up an 8-by-11-inch casserole dish with some olive oil, pour in the elbows and cheeze, cover with foil, and bake for 20 minutes. Meanwhile, stir the bread crumbs and the 2 tablespoons of olive oil together, so that all of the crumbs become coated. If the bread crumbs are unseasoned, add the salt and pepper. If they're already seasoned, do not add salt or pepper. Turn off the oven and set the broiler on high. Top the casserole with the bread-crumb mixture, and toss it under the broiler until the top is browned. This should only take 1 minute or so, so keep an eye on it, because it'll burn very easily.

WTF are panko bread crumbs?

They are a flaky type of bread crumb used in Japanese cooking. Panko are airier than Western-style bread crumbs and have an incredible crunch. They are made from bread that has been "baked" by passing an electric current through the dough (definitely do not try this at home), which makes a bread with no crust. Find them at a Japanese market or in the Asian section of your supermarket.

CRABBY CAKES OVER SUCCOTASH

||||||||||||||||||||||||||||||||||||||||||||||||||||||||||||||||||||||||||||||||||||||||||||||||||||||||||||||||

If, for some lame-o health reasons, you want to sextuple your cooking time by baking these, be my guest. Bake them on a lubed-up baking sheet at 350°F for 30 to 40 minutes, or until they're brown all around. But if I were you, I would just fry them. If you want to serve these as appetizers, make eight smaller cakes instead of four larger ones. As for the side dish, you'll be happy to know that I successfully fought the strong urge to call it "Sufferin' Succotash"...that would've just been corny.

Serves 4

One 8-ounce package tempeh
2 tablespoons plus 2 teaspoons extra-virgin olive oil
¼ cup finely diced yellow onion
¼ cup finely diced celery
¼ cup finely diced red bell pepper
Salt
1 cup panko bread crumbs (see WTF, page 138)
1 tablespoon Old Bay seasoning, plus more for garnish
¼ cup vegan mayo (see WTF, page 42)
One 15-ounce can chickpeas, rinsed and drained until very dry
1 tablespoon capers, drained and chopped
1 tablespoon chopped fresh Italian parsley
2 tablespoons fresh lemon juice
2 teaspoons Dijon mustard
2 teaspoons kelp (or other seaweed) powder (see WTF, page 63)
Hot sauce
Pepper
Succotash (recipe follows)
Remoulade (recipe follows)

Using a steamer basket, steam the tempeh for 25 minutes, then let it cool. While it's steaming, heat the 2 teaspoons of olive oil in a pan over medium heat, and add the onion, celery, bell pepper, and a pinch of salt. Cook until the onions are translucent and tender, about 8 minutes, then set aside to cool. With a fork, potato masher, or your very clean hands, mash the tempeh in a bowl until it's completely "ground." Add the cooked veggies, ½ cup of bread crumbs, ½ tablespoon of Old Bay, the mayo, chickpeas, capers, parsley, lemon juice, mustard, kelp powder, a couple dashes of hot sauce, and a pinch of salt and a pinch of pepper to the tempeh, and mash it all together with your very clean hands until the chickpeas are completely mashed. Divide the chickpea mixture into four 3-inch-wide cakes.

In a large pan, heat the 2 tablespoons of oil over medium-high heat. Mix the remaining ½ cup of bread crumbs with the remaining ½ tablespoon of Old Bay, and spread out on a small plate. Dredge both sides of your cakes in the seasoned bread crumbs. Drop the cakes into the pan and cook for 3 to 4 minutes, or until one side is browned, then flip and brown the other side. Drain the cakes for 1 minute on paper towels, and hit them with a little dash of Old Bay seasoning. Serve over succotash, and top with remoulade.

SUCCOTASH

Serves 4

2 teaspoons vegan margarine
½ cup diced red bell pepper
½ cup diced yellow onion
Salt
1 teaspoon chopped fresh thyme
1 cup white wine
½ cup vegetable stock
½ teaspoon arrowroot dissolved in ¼ teaspoon water
    (see WTF, page 69)

2 cups fresh or frozen corn kernels
1½ cups frozen lima beans
1 tablespoon chopped fresh Italian parsley
Pepper

Heat the margarine in a medium skillet over medium-high heat. When it's melted, add the bell pepper, onion, and a pinch of salt. Cook for 4 to 5 minutes, or until the veggies are soft, and then add the thyme. Cook for 2 more minutes. Add the white wine and let it reduce by half, 2 to 3 minutes, then add the vegetable stock. Bring the stock to a simmer, and whisk in the arrowroot slurry. After cooking for 2 minutes, the sauce will reach maximum thickness (if you want it thicker, add more arrowroot slurry). Add the corn, lima beans, and parsley. Cook until warmed through, about 3 minutes, and season with salt and pepper to taste.

REMOULADE

Store extra remoulade in a sealed container in the fridge for up to a week.

Makes ¾ cup

⅓ cup vegan mayo (see WTF, page 42)
2 scallions, thinly sliced
2 tablespoons Crazy Shit (see recipe, page 194)
1 tablespoon extra-virgin olive oil
2 teaspoons Crazy Shit Vinegar (see recipe, page 194)
1 teaspoon Dijon mustard
1 tablespoon minced fresh Italian parsley
Salt and pepper to taste

Whisk together all ingredients until combined.

GRILLED "FISH" TACOS WITH CORN AND JICAMA SALAD

||||||||||||||||||||||||||||||||||||||||||||||||||||||||||||||||||||||||||||||||||||||||||||||||||||||||||||||||||||||||||||||||

You don't absolutely need to do the freezing-of-the-tofu step, but it does make the "fish" better. If you choose to skip it, just make sure that you drain as much of the water out of the tofu as possible before marinating it. For the Corn and Ji-cama Salad, you could grill the corn, which would be very tasty, but there is nothing better than eating raw, sweet summer corn right off the cob. For most of my life, I thought that corn had to be boiled to death in order for it to be consumed. I have since cut off all communication with those who made me think that. They are dead to me.

Makes 12 tacos (4 to 6 servings)

Two 14-ounce blocks extra-firm tofu, drained (see Tip, page 35), frozen (see Tip, page 136), and thawed

1 cup plus 2 tablespoons fresh lime juice

2 teaspoons seaweed powder (see WTF, page 63)

2 teaspoons chopped fresh cilantro, plus a few sprigs for garnish

¼ teaspoon ground chipotle

½ teaspoon salt

Pepper

Oil for greasing the grill, grill pan, or skillet

¼ cup Sour Creaminess (see recipe, page 205) or other vegan sour cream

¼ cup vegan mayo (see WTF, page 42)

Hot sauce

Twelve 6-inch soft corn tortillas

2 cups finely shredded green cabbage

2 medium Roma tomatoes, diced

4 scallions, thinly sliced

Lime wedges, for garnish

Corn and Jicama Salad (recipe follows)

Scan to watch the video.

Cut both blocks of tofu in half crosswise (when you're cutting, the side of your knife should be parallel with the shorter sides of the tofu block). Then cut the halves into thirds. You should now have 12 flat tofu rectangles — these are your "fish" fillets.

Whisk together the 1 cup of lime juice, the seaweed powder, 2 teaspoons of cilantro, the chipotle, salt, and a pinch of pepper, and put the mixture in a large zip-top bag with the tofu. Gently slosh around so it gets coated, squeeze the bag to suck out as much of the air as possible, and put it in the fridge to marinate for at least 1 hour and up to 4 hours.

Heat your lightly oiled grill, grill pan, or medium skillet over medium heat. Remove the tofu fillets from the marinade and gently shake off the excess. Place them on your grill or in your skillet, and don't touch them for 6 to 8 minutes. When they have grill marks or are browned, flip and cook on the other side for 6 to 8 more minutes. Do this in batches if necessary, keeping the cooked fillets warm in a low oven.

While the tofu is cooking, whisk together the 2 tablespoons of lime juice, the sour creaminess, mayo, and a couple dashes of hot sauce. This is also a good time to warm your tortillas. You can throw them right on the grill or the flame of your gas range and let them heat up until they're pliable.

Transfer the tofu fillets to a cutting board, and cut them into thirds lengthwise. If all those cutting instructions made sense, you should now have pieces that are sort of long cubes, like big fat french fries. (This would be much easier to demonstrate on TV... can someone give me a TV show, please? I promise it will be good. Thank you.)

Spread a bit of the white sauce on a tortilla. Add 3 pieces of tofu, and top with the cabbage, tomato, and scallions. Garnish with the cilantro sprigs and lime wedges. Repeat with the remaining ingredients to make 12 tacos. Serve with Corn and Jicama Salad.

CORN AND JICAMA SALAD

Serves 4 to 6

1 cup raw or grilled corn kernels
1 cup drained freshly cooked or rinsed canned black beans
1 cup diced peeled jicama
1 cup shredded carrot
2 scallions, thinly sliced
2 tablespoons roasted pepitas (see WTF, page 56)
2 tablespoons chopped fresh cilantro
1 tablespoon fresh basil chiffonade (see WTF, page 103)
¼ cup extra-virgin olive oil
1 tablespoon fresh lime juice
¼ cup fresh orange juice
Zest of 2 limes
¼ teaspoon ground cumin
¼ teaspoon ground coriander
Salt and pepper

In a medium bowl, combine the corn, beans, jicama, carrot, scallions, pepitas, cilantro, and basil.

In another medium bowl, whisk together the oil, lime juice, orange juice, lime zest, cumin, and coriander. Toss with the veggies. Season with salt and pepper to taste.

SEITAN STEAK 'N' FRIES

|||||||||||||||||||||||||||||||||||||||||||||||||||||||||||||||||||||||||||||||||||||||||||||||||||||||||||||

This is a re-creation of my "last supper" — the final meal I ate before I transitioned into enlightenment, the last time I consumed meat of any kind. I'm not waxing poetic here, but it happened to be a great meal then, and it's a *better* meal now. I've replaced dead cow with seitan, and where there were roasted potatoes, there are now celery root oven fries. The gravy remains the same. This is one to serve to that veg-curious friend who needs one last push. And look, if some of that gravy makes its way onto those oven fries, it is not going to hurt anyone.

Serves 4

4 tablespoons extra-virgin olive oil
8 Basic Seitan Cutlets (see recipe, pages 24–25)
4 teaspoons Blackened Seasoning (see recipe, page 210)
¼ cup diced yellow onion
1 cup thickly sliced cremini or button mushrooms
Salt
1 clove garlic, minced
½ teaspoon chopped fresh thyme
½ teaspoon chopped fresh sage
2 tablespoons unbleached all-purpose flour
2 teaspoons nutritional yeast (see WTF, page 27)
2 teaspoons low-sodium tamari or soy sauce (see WTF, page 25)
½ cup white wine
2 cups vegetable stock, heated
Pinch of celery seed (optional)
1 tablespoon chopped fresh Italian parsley, for garnish
Celery Root Oven Fries (recipe follows)

In a large, high-sided skillet, heat 1 tablespoon of the oil over high heat. Rub another tablespoon of oil on the seitan cutlets, and generously coat both sides with the blackened seasoning. Slowly place one cutlet in the skillet. If you don't hear a sizzle, wait until the oil in the skillet gets hotter. If it does sizzle, place all cutlets in the skillet (do it in batches if you need to). Fry the seitan on one side for 3 minutes, or until browned, then flip and repeat. When the second side is browned, remove the cutlets from the pan and set aside.

To the same pan, add the remaining 2 tablespoons of oil, and lower the heat to medium. Add the onion, mushrooms, and a pinch of salt, and cook for 4 minutes. Add the garlic, thyme, and sage, and cook for 4 more minutes, or until the mushrooms are soft and the onion is tender and translucent. Stir in the flour. Continue stirring for 5 minutes, until the flour becomes a blond color, then add the nutritional yeast, tamari, and wine. Cook for 2 more minutes, then stir in ½ cup of the heated stock. When the liquid is incorporated, stir in the rest of the stock ½ cup at a time. Adding the stock in stages prevents a lumpy gravy. Stir in the celery seed, if using, return the seitan cutlets to the pan, and submerge them in the gravy. Gently simmer for 5 more minutes. Place two cutlets on each plate, top with the gravy, garnish with parsley, and serve with a side of celery root oven fries.

CELERY ROOT OVEN FRIES

Serves 4

3 teaspoons extra-virgin olive oil
2 pounds celery root, peeled and cut into steak-fry shapes
Salt and pepper

Preheat the oven to 350°F. Line a baking sheet with foil and lube up the foil with 1 teaspoon of oil. In a large bowl, toss the celery root with the remaining 2 teaspoons of oil, a healthy pinch of salt, and a couple grinds of pepper. Spread out the celery root fries on the baking sheet and bake for 1 hour, tossing after 30 minutes. Remove from the oven and taste. Season with salt and pepper if needed.

Scan to watch
the video.

MEXICALI QUINOA WITH BLACK LENTILS AND PRETEND CHIPOTLE SAUSAGES

||||||||||||||||||||||||||||||||||||||||||||||||||||||||||||||||||||||||||||||||||||||||||||||||

This is a protein-packed twist on rice 'n' beans. To be honest, I didn't even think of it that way when I formulated it. I just put shit together that sounded good. When I served it to the Girlfriend, she said, "Oh, I see, it's like black beans and rice. You're so smart!" And I said, "Ummm…no, *you're* so smart for figuring out my clever play on a classic Mexican dish."

Serves 4

1 cup black lentils
2 cups water, plus more if needed
Pinch of ground cumin
Pinch of ground coriander
Salt and pepper
4 teaspoons extra-virgin olive oil
½ cup diced yellow onion
½ cup diced carrot
½ cup diced celery
2 cloves garlic, minced
1 tablespoon tomato paste
1 cup quinoa, rinsed thoroughly (see Tip, page 45)
2 cups vegetable stock
1 teaspoon chopped fresh cilantro, plus more for garnish
¼ cup frozen corn kernels
¼ cup frozen peas
8 Pretend Chipotle Sausages (see recipe, page 29)
Pico de Gallo, for garnish (see recipe, page 187)
Gargantuan Guac, for garnish (see recipe, page 183)

In a small pot, cover the lentils with the 2 cups of water. Bring to a boil, then lower to a simmer, and cover. Cook for 20 to 25 minutes, checking periodically to make sure the water hasn't completely evaporated. If the water evaporates before the lentils are cooked, add a little more. The key is to keep the lentils just barely covered. When the lentils get soft, season with the cumin, coriander, and salt and pepper to taste. Then mash them with the back of a wooden spoon until they get to a "refried bean" consistency. If you need to add more water to get the right consistency, that's totally cool. Season with more salt and pepper if needed, and they're done.

In a small pot, heat 2 teaspoons of the oil over medium heat. Add the onion, carrot, celery, and a pinch of salt. Cook for 4 to 6 minutes, or until the veggies are softened. Then stir in the garlic and the tomato paste, and cook for 2 more minutes. Stir in the quinoa and cook, stirring, for 1 more minute. Stir in the vegetable stock. Cover and simmer for 10 to 12 minutes, or until all the liquid is absorbed and the quinoa is soft. Finally, stir in the ½ teaspoon of cilantro, the corn, and peas. Turn off the heat, and cover for 4 minutes.

Heat a grill, grill pan, or medium skillet over medium-high heat. Coat the sausages with the remaining 2 teaspoons of oil, and place on the hot grill or skillet. Let brown for 2 to 3 minutes, then flip and brown on the other side, 2 to 3 more minutes. Cut the sausages in half, on the diagonal. To serve, place a couple spoonfuls of quinoa on each plate, spreading it in a ¼-inch-thick layer. Top the quinoa with a big spoonful of the black lentils, and then fancily place 4 sausage halves on top of the lentils. Garnish with pico de gallo, guac, and cilantro.

JAMBALAYA

||||||||||||||||||||||||||||||||||||||||||||||||||||||||||||||||||||||||||||||||||||||||||||||||||||||||||

You might as well spare your door frame and unlock your front door when you make this jambalaya, because your neighbors will stop at nothing to get some of it when those aromas start wafting. (Heh, *wafting* — that word always makes me think about fanning farts into my brothers' faces.)

Serves 4

4 teaspoons extra-virgin olive oil
1 cup diced celery
1 cup diced red bell pepper
1 cup diced yellow onion
3 cloves garlic, minced
Salt
1 teaspoon dried thyme
¼ teaspoon cayenne
½ teaspoon dried oregano
½ teaspoon onion powder
½ teaspoon paprika
One 28-ounce can crushed tomatoes
4 Pretend Chipotle Sausages (see recipe, page 29)
Pepper
4 cups cooked brown rice
1 tablespoon chopped fresh Italian parsley, for garnish

In a pot, heat 2 teaspoons of the oil over medium heat. Add the celery, bell pepper, onion, garlic, and a pinch of salt, and cook for 6 to 8 minutes, or until the veggies are soft. Add the thyme, cayenne, oregano, onion powder, and paprika, and stir to coat the veggies. Cook for 2 more minutes. Stir in the tomatoes, lower the heat to medium-low, and simmer, stirring occasionally, for 20 minutes.

Meanwhile, heat a grill, grill pan, or medium skillet over medium-high heat. Coat the sausages with the remaining 2 teaspoons of oil, and place on the hot grill or skillet. Let brown for 2 to 3 minutes, then flip and brown on the other side, 2 to 3 minutes. Cut the sausages on the diagonal into ¼-inch-thick slices.

When the sauce is done, season with salt and pepper to taste. To serve, place rice in the bottom of each bowl, ladle some sauce over the rice, and top with the sausages. Garnish with the parsley.

SHEPHERD'S PIE

||||||||||||||||||||||||||||||||||||||||||||||||||||||||||||||||||||||||||||||||||||||||||||||||||||||||||||||||||||||||||||||||||||||||||||||

This is for those blustery winter eves, when you come in from the cold, kick off your snow boots, and have your dinner while warming your feet by the crackling fire. I don't have winter in Southern California, so I just sit at my table as usual. If I could figure out how to turn on my gas fireplace with the fake logs, I'd at least do that...but that has proven difficult thus far.

Serves 6 to 8

1 tablespoon extra-virgin olive oil
1 cup diced yellow onion
1 cup diced celery
1 cup diced carrot
1 cup diced fennel
2 cups roughly chopped cremini mushrooms
3 cloves garlic, chopped
Salt and pepper
¾ cup green lentils
½ cup vegan dark beer (see Tip, next page)
1½ cups vegetable stock, plus more if needed
2 teaspoons vegan Worcestershire sauce (see WTF, page 12)
¼ cup frozen peas
Mashed Taters (see recipe, page 134)
2 pinches paprika

Preheat the oven to 350°F. In a large pot or pan, heat the oil over medium-high heat. Add the onion, celery, carrot, fennel, mushrooms, garlic, and a healthy pinch of salt. Cook for 5 to 7 minutes, or until the veggies are soft. Next, stir in the lentils, add the beer, and let simmer for about 3 minutes. Then add the vegetable stock and Worcestershire, bring to a simmer, and cover. Let simmer for 15 to 20 minutes. Check it from time to time to make sure that the liquid hasn't evaporated. If, when you check it, the lentils are no longer covered by liquid, add a little more stock.

When the lentils are soft, you're good to go. Turn off the heat, and with a potato masher or the back of a wooden spoon, mash the lentil mixture a little bit. Not into complete mush, just until the liquid thickens. Finally, stir in the peas, and season with salt and pepper to taste.

Transfer the stew to a large casserole dish, and evenly spread the mashed taters over the top. Cover with foil, and bake for 10 to 15 minutes, or until the taters are warmed through. Remove the foil, sprinkle the top with the paprika, and broil on high for 2 to 3 minutes, or until the potatoes are browned. Let stand 5 minutes, then serve.

TIP

I used to think that beer was basically just plants and water, and therefore always vegan. This is not true. Some beers are processed with enzymes extracted from fish bladders, or something to that effect. On the very useful website Barnivore.com, you can find out which booze is vegan and which is not. Ohhhhh, I get it — bar-nivore, like you're at a bar where there's booze…barnivore, ah, very good.

CHAPTER 8

pizza!!

PIZZA IS AMAZING! It has a crust. A crust that can be thick and chewy, or thin and crispy. It can be infused with herbs and spices and may be created from any combination of grains that your heart desires. It can be stretched to feed an army or cut down to feed one person. Its sauce can be sweet, savory, mild, or spicy, and it can range in color from white to barbecue. Its topping possibilities are as infinite as the amount of time the *USS Enterprise D* would have remained in that tachyon distortion time-loop thing had Data not chosen to obey Riker's command over Picard's. Pizza is my inspiration in my work, and in my life. If we could all have the flexibility, versatility, and balance that pizza has, I think there's nothing we wouldn't be able to do as a people. Pretty awesome stuff.

I have one piece of advice before we start with the pizzas: GET A PIZZA STONE! It is a flat firebrick stone that mimics the hot surface of a pizzeria oven. It'll cost you about 40 bucks and last a lifetime. Using it is easy, but you do need to preheat it for 40 minutes or so at 450°F. All the pizzas in this chapter are baked at 450°F as well.

You should also get a pizza peel, which is that giant spatula they use to take the pizzas in and out of the ovens. I know I'm asking you to shell out some additional cash, but I wouldn't do so unless I really thought it mattered. These tips will maximize your pizza-ing experience. You're welcome.

BASIC PIZZA DOUGH

||||||||||||||||||||||||||||||||||||||||||||||||||||||||||||||||||||||||||||||||||||||||||||||||||||||||||

Pizza dough is the one place where my efforts to have maximum nutrition in everything I eat are kinda tossed out the window. You can certainly substitute 1 cup of whole-wheat flour in this recipe if you want to, but when it comes to pizza, I like a good old-fashioned white-flour crust under my sauce and toppings.

The following is a basic dough recipe that you can mold to your fancy. For the purposes of the rest of the recipes in this chapter, this recipe makes 3 "pizza doughs." So when I say "1 pizza dough, rolled out to a 14-inch diameter." I'm saying to use one-third of the dough that this recipe yields.

Makes three 14-inch thin pizza crusts

1 cup warm water
2¼ teaspoons or one 7 g package active dry yeast
1 tablespoon extra-virgin olive oil, plus more as needed and
    to coat the bowl and dough
1 tablespoon agave nectar
Salt
3 cups unbleached all-purpose flour, plus more for dusting
    the work surface

In a bowl, combine the water, yeast, the 1 tablespoon of oil, agave nectar, and a healthy pinch of salt. Gently mix it all together and let it sit for 5 minutes, until it starts to froth. This ensures the yeast is active and has not expired. Add 2 cups of the flour, and mix it up (I do it by hand, but you could use a stand mixer with a dough hook). Continue to slowly add the rest of the flour until you have a slightly sticky ball. Then knead the dough by hand or in your stand mixer. You can add a little flour if the dough starts to stick to your hands. You'll need to knead the dough until it is smooth and elastic; this will take about 10 minutes by hand (or 5 minutes on medium speed if you're using a stand mixer). After kneading, form it into a ball.

Coat a large bowl with oil. (The dough is going to double in size in that bowl, so make sure the bowl is big enough.) Also coat the dough with olive oil. Put the dough in the bowl, cover it with a damp kitchen towel, and stash it someplace warm for 90 minutes for its first rise. I find that turning my oven on to 200°F for 2 minutes, then turning it off, creates the perfect environment for rising dough. After the first rise, give the dough a couple of light, open-handed slaps to make it collapse so that it's flattened out. Then let it rise for 40 more minutes. To make three 14-inch thin-crust pizzas, divide the dough into thirds. If you like a thicker crust, use half of the dough instead of a third for each pie. PIZZA TIME!!!

Mangia!!!

THE MARIO

||||||||||||||||||||||||||||||||||||||||||||||||||||||||||||||||||||||||||||||||||||||||||||||||||||||||||

There have been two great Italian men in my life. From the time I was a little boy, they showed me many things. From basic activities, such as running and jumping, to advanced life skills, like using turtle shells as weapons and punching bricks in a way that makes them yield coins and mushrooms, these two guys gave me an education I could never get in school. In fact, I often neglected my schoolwork in favor of hanging out with them...but I turned out kind of okay anyway. The first two pizzas of this chapter are dedicated to, and named after, my great Italian mentors.

Makes one 14-inch pizza

½ recipe Caponata (see recipe, page 130)
1 Basic Pizza Dough (see recipe, page 158), rolled out to a
    14-inch diameter
1 cup Not-zzarella Sauce (see recipe, page 214) or other
    vegan cheese
1 small handful baby arugula, for garnish
2 teaspoons Parmesan Topping (see recipe, page 211)
1 tablespoon Balsamic Glaze (see recipe, page 199)

Preheat the oven to 450°F. Spread the caponata evenly across the pizza dough. Then add the not-zzarella sauce (using a squeeze bottle to do this in a fancy spiral fashion is pretty sweet, so try that). Bake for 7 to 9 minutes, or until the crust browns. Remove from the oven, and top with the arugula leaves and parmesan topping. Finally, drizzle on the balsamic glaze in an artful manner.

THE LUIGI

|||||||||||||||||||||||||||||||||||||||||||||||||||||||||||||||||||||||||||||||||||||||||||||||||||||||||

Makes one 14-inch pizza

2 cups extra-virgin olive oil
20 cloves garlic
Salt
3 leaves kale, stemmed and coarsely chopped
1 cup Cashew Ricotta (see recipe, page 213)
1 Basic Pizza Dough (see recipe, page 158), rolled out to a
    14-inch diameter
1 cup Not-zzarella Sauce (see recipe, page 214) or other
    vegan cheese
2 teaspoons Parmesan Topping (see recipe, page 211)
1 tablespoon fresh basil chiffonade (see WTF, page 103)

Preheat the oven to 450°F. Put the olive oil and garlic in a small pot. Make sure there is enough oil to completely submerge the garlic cloves. Gently simmer the cloves in the oil over medium heat for 10 to 15 minutes, or until slightly browned and soft. Turn off the heat, and when the oil cools, remove the cloves and set aside. You also now have garlic oil, which is very tasty, so store it in a sealed container or mason jar in the fridge for up to a week. You can use it in place of olive oil in salad dressings and sauces.

Prepare an ice bath by adding cold water and ice cubes to a wide bowl. Bring a small pot of water to a boil. Add a healthy pinch of salt, and drop in the kale. Let cook for 30 seconds, remove, and cool immediately in the ice bath. When it's cooled, remove the kale from the ice bath with a slotted spoon, squeeze out as much water as possible, and set aside.

Spread the ricotta evenly across the pizza dough. Then add the not-zzarella sauce (using a squeeze bottle to do this in a fancy spiral fashion is pretty sweet, so try that). Top with the kale and the roasted garlic cloves. Bake for 7 to 9 minutes, or until the crust browns. Top with the parmesan topping and the basil.

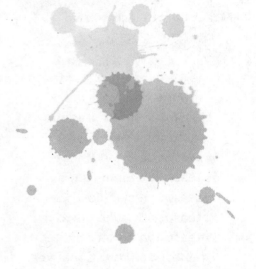

PRETEND SAUSAGE AND PEPPERS

||||||||||||||||||||||||||||||||||||||||||||||||||||||||||||||||||||||||||||||||||||||||||||||||||||||||||||||

This is a classic combo that takes me way back. Reminds me of that fat little 12-year-old who was terrible at every sport, played video games all day, and couldn't get that one girl to like him. I used to beat the crap out of that kid, take his lunch money, and go buy a sausage-and-pepper slice with it. I hope he's doing all right now.

Makes one 14-inch pizza

- One 14-ounce block extra-firm tofu, drained (see Tip, page 35)
- 1 teaspoon dried oregano
- 1 teaspoon dried basil
- ½ teaspoon dried thyme
- ½ teaspoon fennel seeds
- ¼ teaspoon chili flakes
- ½ teaspoon garlic powder
- ½ teaspoon onion powder
- 1 tablespoon nutritional yeast (see WTF, page 27)
- ¼ teaspoon salt
- 1 tablespoon extra-virgin olive oil, plus more for coating the baking dish
- 1 teaspoon vegan Worcestershire sauce (see WTF, page 12)
- 1 red bell pepper, sliced
- ½ yellow onion, sliced
- ¾ cup Tomato Killer (see recipe, page 200) or other tomato sauce
- 1 Basic Pizza Dough (see recipe, page 158), rolled out to 14-inch diameter
- 1 cup Not-zzarella Sauce (see recipe, page 211) or other vegan cheese
- Parmesan Topping (see recipe, page 211)
- 6 leaves fresh basil, torn

Preheat the oven to 400°F. In a large bowl, combine the tofu, oregano, basil, thyme, fennel, chili flakes, garlic powder, onion powder, nutritional yeast, salt, the 1 tablespoon of olive oil, and the Worcestershire. With your very clean hands, blend the ingredients by mashing the tofu until it is completely broken up into a ground meat–like texture. Then mix in the bell pepper and onion. Lube up a casserole or baking dish with some olive oil, and spread the tofu mixture evenly in the dish. To ensure that it browns properly, make sure the layer is no more than ½ inch thick, using a second dish if necessary.

Bake the mixture for 30 minutes, then remove it from the oven. The top of the mixture should be lightly browned at this point. Toss it around with a spatula to allow the other side to brown. Return the mixture to the oven, and cook for 30 more minutes, or until the mixture is mostly browned with some moist, white tofu-looking parts remaining. Set aside to cool.

Raise the oven temperature to 450°F. Spread the tomato killer evenly across the dough, and top it with the not-zzarella sauce, then the cooked tofu mixture. Bake in the oven for 7 to 9 minutes, or until the crust begins to brown. Remove from the oven, and top with a sprinkle of parmesan topping and the basil.

THE B.L.A.T.

||||||||||||||||||||||||||||||||||||||||||||||||||||||||||||||||||||||||||||||||||||||||||||||||||||||||||||||||||||||||||||||

It's a great sandwich, so why not a pizza?

Makes one 14-inch pizza

1½ cups Smoked Cheddar Sauce (see recipe, page 215)
1 Basic Pizza Dough (see recipe, page 158), rolled out to a
   14-inch diameter
1 beefsteak tomato, thinly sliced
Salt
8 strips Tempeh Bacon (see recipe, page 32), chopped
½ medium avocado, thinly sliced
1 small handful watercress

Preheat the oven to 450°F. Spread the smoked cheddar sauce evenly across the dough. Add the tomato slices and hit them with a pinch of salt. Add the bacon, and bake for 7 to 9 minutes. Take the pizza out of the oven, and arrange the avocado slices on top in an elegant, symmetrical manner. Finally, top with the watercress.

THREE-CHEEZE PESTO

||||||||||||||||||||||||||||||||||||||||||||||||||||||||||||||||||||||||||||||||||||||||||||||||||||||||||||||||

I must take this moment to talk to you about a thing called "pine mouth." This is a thing that sucks majorly. There are distributors of pine nuts around the world that have started packaging an inedible breed of pine nut as edible. They look, taste, and feel just like regular pine nuts, but some people have a very unpleasant reaction to them: after eating them, they get a lingering bitter, metallic taste in their mouths and everything they eat tastes terrible. This happened to me when I was testing this pizza. Do your own research on this "pine mouth" syndrome, and if you don't trust the pine nuts in your area, sub in raw walnuts or cashews for your pesto sauces.

Makes one 14-inch pizza

2 tablespoons raw pine nuts (if you dare)
1 cup Basil Pesto (see recipe, page 217)
1 Basic Pizza Dough (see recipe, page 158), rolled out to a
    14-inch diameter
1 cup Cashew Ricotta (see recipe, page 213)
1 cup Not-zzarella Sauce (see recipe, page 214) or other
    vegan cheese
2 teaspoons Parmesan Topping (see recipe, page 211)
1 tablespoon fresh basil chiffonade (see WTF, page 103)
Extra-virgin olive oil for drizzling (optional)

Preheat the oven to 450°F. To toast the pine nuts, heat a dry pan over medium-high heat and cook the pine nuts for 1 to 2 minutes on one side, until they're slightly browned, then toss and cook for another 30 to 60 seconds (keep a close eye on them — they burn super easily). Set aside.

Spread the pesto evenly across the pizza dough. Then spread the ricotta over that, and top it with the not-zzarella sauce (again, it's always sweet to use a squeeze bottle to get that fancy spiral design). Bake for 7 to 9 minutes, or until the crust browns. Top it with the pine nuts, parmesan topping, basil, and a little drizzle of olive oil.

THE MUSH-A-BOKI
||||||||||||||||||||||||||||||||||||||||||||||||||||||||||||||||||||||||||||||||||||||||||||||||||||||||||||||||||||

This is what my dad calls mushrooms. I guess he just made it up.

Me: "Hey Dad, we're ordering pizza (again), what do you want on it? I'm thinking sweet peppers."

Dad: "What, no mush-a-bokis?"

Me: "Oh yeah, let's do that."

Dad: "How 'bout some pepperovich too?"

I can't believe I almost forgot about that one. "Pepperoni" was known as "pepperovich." Never thought about it until now, but my dad is a pretty prolific pizza-topping renamer.

Makes one 14-inch pizza

2 teaspoons extra-virgin olive oil
8 ounces fresh shiitake mushrooms, stemmed and sliced
8 ounces fresh cremini mushrooms, halved
1 teaspoon chopped fresh thyme
Salt and pepper
3½ ounces fresh enoki mushrooms, bottoms trimmed, cut into
    1-inch pieces
¼ cup dry white wine (or, if you wanna get nuts, use sake)
3 packed cups baby spinach
1 lemon wedge
1 cup Cashew Ricotta (see recipe, page 213)
1 Basic Pizza Dough (see recipe, page 158), rolled out to a
    14-inch diameter
1 cup Not-zzarella Sauce (see recipe, page 214) or other
    vegan cheese
2 teaspoons Parmesan Topping (see recipe, page 211)
2 teaspoons fresh basil chiffonade (see WTF, page 103)

Preheat the oven to 450°F. In a large skillet, heat the oil over medium heat. Add the shiitakes and creminis. Cook for 4 to 6 minutes, or until browned, then add the thyme and a pinch of salt and a pinch of pepper. Cook for 2 to 3 more minutes, and push them off to the side of the pan. Add the enokis, and cook for 1 to 3 minutes, until browned on one side, then toss them with the rest of the mushrooms. Stir in the wine, and let it reduce until it's almost all evaporated, 1 to 2 minutes. Finally, add the spinach to the pan and toss it with the mushrooms until wilted. Squeeze just a spritz of lemon juice into the mixture, season with salt and pepper, and set aside to cool.

Spread the ricotta evenly across the dough. Then top that with a layer of the not-zzarella sauce (if you can make fancy swirls of it with a squeeze bottle, all the better), and top that with the mushroom-spinach mixture. Bake in the oven for 7 to 9 minutes, or until the crust begins to brown. Remove from the oven, and top with the parmesan topping and basil.

CHAPTER 9

snackage

SNACKS! YES!! VERY EXCITING!! This is the one meal that we can all get behind. While a lot of us don't care so much for breakfast or put a whole lot of time into planning lunch or dinner (some issues that I have hopefully resolved with this book), the little bites in between these meals (or way, way after them) are the ones that we, as a people, have been most passionate about. Whether it's to tide you over before a late dinner date or to sate a ravenous case of the post-boozing munchies, this chapter has what you need. Chow down!

NACHOS VENTI

That's bigger than "grande," right?

Makes 1 large platter

2 cups Not Yo Mama's Cheeze Sauce (see recipe, page 216)
2 cups Chili Topping (see recipe, page 206)
10 to 12 ounces tortilla chips
2 cups drained freshly cooked black beans or one 15-ounce
    can black beans, rinsed and drained
½ cup Sour Creaminess (see recipe, page 205) or other vegan
    sour cream
1 cup Pico de Gallo (see recipe, page 187)
1 medium avocado, diced
½ cup thinly sliced scallions
Cilantro sprigs, for garnish

Can't believe I'm about to explain the construction of nachos, but I must be thorough: Gently heat the cheeze sauce and the chili topping in separate pots, until they're very warm. We're gonna do this in two layers, because, well, why wouldn't you? Since we won't be placing the entire thing in the oven, I actually like to put the chips on a baking sheet and warm them in the oven at a low temp (about 200°F) for about 5 minutes. On your serving platter, spread out half of the chips and top with half of the chili mixture. Top that with half of the beans, and top it all with half of the cheeze sauce. Now add the rest of your chips and do the same chili-bean-cheeze process as with the first layer. Finally, top the whole thing with a few strategically placed dollops of sour cream, the pico de gallo, avocado, and scallions. Garnish with cilantro sprigs.

TATER SKINZ

||||||||||||||||||||||||||||||||||||||||||||||||||||||||||||||||||||||||||||||||||||||||||||||||||||||||||||||||||||

Things are much cooler when you replace an s with a z. Just ask Jay-Z — his original last name was S. Just imagine if he'd kept it.

Serves 4

2 large russet potatoes
2 teaspoons extra-virgin olive oil
Salt and pepper
8 strips Tempeh Bacon, chopped into bits (see recipe,
    page 32)
4 tablespoons Smoked Cheddar Sauce (see recipe, page 215)
4 tablespoons Sour Creaminess (see recipe, page 205) or
    other vegan sour cream
½ cup diced seeded tomato (see Tip, next page)
1 scallion, thinly sliced

Preheat the oven to 350°F. Pierce the potatoes a few times with a fork, coat with 1 teaspoon of the oil, and season with salt and pepper. Bake for 75 to 90 minutes. When you can easily insert a fork or toothpick all the way to the middle, they're ready. Remove from the oven and let cool.

Turn off the oven and set your broiler on high. When the potatoes are cool enough to handle, cut them in half lengthwise, and scoop out the flesh, leaving a ¼-inch layer still attached to the skin. Save the flesh to make gnocchi or to stir into soup as a thickener. Rub the inside of the potatoes with the remaining 1 teaspoon of oil, salt, and pepper. Place the potatoes, flesh side up, under the broiler for 1 to 3 minutes, or until browned. Remove them from the broiler, and top each of the skinz with one-quarter of the bacon bits, and top that with 1 tablespoon of cheddar cheeze sauce. Place the skinz back under the broiler for 1 to 2 minutes, or until the cheddar sauce begins to brown and bubble. Take them out of the oven and top each with 1 tablespoon of sour creaminess, 2 tablespoons of tomato, and a few scallions.

TIP

To seed a tomato, cut the tomato into quarters lengthwise, thus exposing the pockets of seeds. Run a paring knife along the inner flesh of the tomato, just under the seeds. Discard the seeds and gel-like substance around them.

CREAMY ONION DIP

||||||||||||||||||||||||||||||||||||||||||||||||||||||||||||||||||||||||||||||||||||||||||||||||||||||||||||||||||||||||||

Ahem...serve this dip with a healthy, elegant assortment of fresh vegetables... pffft, who are we kidding? Polish it off with a family-size bag of potato chips, crack some brew-dogs, and yell at the sports players through your TV. I'm so manly.

Makes 2 cups

2 teaspoons extra-virgin olive oil
2 cups diced yellow onion
Salt
2 cloves garlic, sliced
½ teaspoon chopped fresh thyme
1½ teaspoons brown sugar
1 cup Sour Creaminess (see recipe, page 205) or other vegan
    sour cream
1 tablespoon vegan mayo (see WTF, page 42)
1 teaspoon chopped fresh Italian parsley
Pepper

In a frying pan, heat the oil over medium heat. Add the onion and a pinch of salt, and give it a quick stir. Let the onion cook for 3 to 4 minutes on one side, then stir and let cook for 3 more minutes. Stir in the garlic and thyme, and cook for 2 more minutes. Lower the heat to medium-low, and stir in the brown sugar. Let this mixture slowly cook for 15 to 20 more minutes, stirring occasionally. When the onions are soft and caramelized, they're ready. Let them cool.

In a food processor or blender, combine the onion mixture, sour creaminess, mayo, and parsley. Blend until smooth. Season with salt and pepper to taste.

GOLDEN BEET HUMMUS

Scan to watch
the video.

If you leave the beets out of this one, you'll have a basic hummus that can act as a blank flavor canvas. You also may need a little more water to get the desired consistency. Add olives, sundried tomatoes, roasted peppers (as shown in the corresponding video), or any number of spices, like cumin or smoked paprika. Serve the hummus with pita or fresh veggies, or on a sandwich, in a wrap, or in your cereal...just making sure you were still paying attention. Seriously, though, this stuff is good on just about anything.

Makes 2 cups

2 baby golden beets (about 4 ounces), greens removed and
   bottoms trimmed
2 teaspoons extra-virgin olive oil
Salt and pepper
One 15-ounce can chickpeas, rinsed and drained
4 teaspoons fresh lemon juice
¼ cup water
1 tablespoon tahini
1 clove garlic

Scan to watch
the video.

Preheat the oven to 350°F. Toss the beets with olive oil and a pinch of salt and a pinch of pepper. Individually wrap the beets in foil, leaving a little opening for steam to escape. Roast the beets for 1 hour, or until a fork easily pierces them. Remove the beets from the foil, and when they are cool enough to handle, scrape off their skins with a small spoon. Cut the beets into quarters.

In a food processor or blender, combine the beets, chickpeas, lemon juice, water, tahini, and garlic, and blend until smooth. Season with salt and pepper to taste.

BUFFALO WANGS

|||||||||||||||||||||||||||||||||||||||||||||||||||||||||||||||||||||||||||||||||||||||||||||||||||||||||||||

The reason for using potato chips as the coating for these bad boys is threefold. Fold 1: chips are crunchy. Fold 2: they are already evenly coated in oil. And the third and final fold: they are perfectly seasoned. I recommend using the thickest chip possible, as it makes for a very hearty coating for that sauce to stick to. A vegan blue cheese dressing has eluded me thus far; however the dressing for the Grilled Cobb salad (see recipe, page 84) will work very well here. Okay, let's get wangin'!

Makes 12 wangs

1 recipe Basic Seitan dough, uncooked (see recipe, page 24)
1 teaspoon extra-virgin olive oil
1 cup ground crinkle-cut or "ruffled" potato chips (ground in a
    food processor or blender)
½ cup unbleached all-purpose flour
½ cup water
¼ cup vegan margarine
¼ cup your favorite hot sauce
1 teaspoon arrowroot dissolved in ½ teaspoon water
    (see WTF, page 69)
Salt and pepper
1 stalk celery, cut into six 3-inch spears, with one pointed end
1 carrot, cut into six 3-inch spears, with one pointed end

Scan to watch
the video.

Divide the uncooked seitan dough into 12 pieces. Roll each piece into a football-like shape and wrap individually in foil, leaving a little room for the dough to expand but making the packet tight enough that the foil will not open as it expands. Using a steamer basket, steam for 45 minutes, then remove the dough from the foil and let cool.

Preheat the oven to 450°F. Have a baking sheet lined with foil and lubed up with 1 teaspoon of oil standing by. On a wide plate, spread the ground potato chips. In a small bowl, whisk together the flour and water to make a batter. Dip each piece of seitan in the batter, let the excess fall away, dredge both sides in the potato chips until well coated, and place on the baking sheet. When all the pieces are coated, bake them for 20 minutes, or until golden.

In a small pot, melt the margarine over low heat. When it's melted, whisk in the hot sauce, and bring to a simmer. Whisk in the arrowroot slurry to thicken your sauce. If you want it thicker, add more arrowroot slurry. Season with salt and pepper to taste. Toss the browned seitan with the sauce, then insert the pointed ends of the celery and carrot spears into the seitan pieces to use as handles.

BOOMIN' SHROOMERS

||||||||||||||||||||||||||||||||||||||||||||||||||||||||||||||||||||||||||||||||||||||||||||||||||||||||||||||||||||||||||

These marinated mushrooms are so friggin' easy to make, and you can use any combination of mushrooms you like. Just make sure that all the mushrooms are cut to roughly the same size. This ensures even flavor penetration and softening.

Serves 4

8 ounces cremini or other mushrooms, halved or left whole
¼ cup fresh lemon juice
¼ cup extra-virgin olive oil
2 cloves garlic, minced
1 teaspoon chopped fresh oregano
½ teaspoon chopped fresh thyme
2 teaspoons chopped fresh Italian parsley
Pinch of chili flakes
½ teaspoon salt
Pepper to taste

Place all ingredients in a zip-top bag. Mix them together thoroughly, squeeze the bag to suck out as much of the excess air as possible, and refrigerate for a minimum of 12 hours — the longer, the better. To serve, pour all of the contents of the bag into a large bowl and let come to room temperature.

GARGANTUAN GUAC

||||||||||||||||||||||||||||||||||||||||||||||||||||||||||||||||||||||||||||||||||||||||||||||||||||||||||

When it comes to guacamole, you just can't beat homemade. You can't. Go ahead, try it. I dare you! Well, c'mon! Bring it! Uh-huh, that's what I thought. Bee-otch!

Scan to watch the video.

Makes 2 cups

2 medium avocados
¼ cup diced red onion
1 serrano pepper or ½ jalapeno pepper, seeded and minced, (see Tip, page 185)
2 tablespoons chopped fresh cilantro
Juice of 1 lime
1 Roma tomato, seeded and diced
Salt and pepper

TIP
HTF do I store this guac?

While we humans need oxygen to survive, the avocado is all like, "Step off, oxygen. I prefer you not be here." Oxidation is what makes avocados, and in turn guacamole, turn brown. So the less oxygen it touches, the better. You can extend the life of your guac by transferring leftovers to an airtight container. Before you put the lid on, spritz the top with fresh lime juice, then place a piece of plastic wrap directly on the guac, and press it so that there is no air touching the guac. It will last in the fridge like this for 2 to 3 days.

Cut the avocados in half lengthwise, rotating your knife around the pits. Separate the halves and remove the pits. With a big spoon, scoop out all the flesh and put it in a bowl. Discard the peel. Add the onion, serrano or jalapeno pepper, cilantro, and lime juice, and mash together with a fork, a potato masher, or your very clean hands. Gently fold in the tomato, and season with salt and pepper to taste.

JALAPENO POPPERS

||||||||||||||||||||||||||||||||||||||||||||||||||||||||||||||||||||||||||||||||||||||||||||||||||||

I suppose you could deep-fry these little guys, but they actually come out crunchier and more evenly cooked in the oven. So that is my preference. For the bread crumbs, I like to use a mix of regular and panko (see WTF, page 138).

Makes 20 poppers

1 cup whole raw walnuts
2 tablespoons nutritional yeast (see WTF, page 27)
¼ teaspoon garlic powder
¼ teaspoon onion powder
¼ teaspoon turmeric
½ teaspoon paprika
Pinch of ground chipotle
¼ teaspoon mustard powder
¼ teaspoon salt, plus more as needed
2 tablespoons extra-virgin olive oil
½ teaspoon yellow miso
4 tablespoons water
⅓ cup canned mild green chilis (either whole or diced)
Pepper
10 jalapeno peppers, halved lengthwise and seeded (see Tip, next page)
¾ cup unbleached all-purpose flour
¾ cup unsweetened nondairy milk
2 cups bread crumbs
Oil or cooking spray, for spritzing

Preheat the oven to 400°F. In a food processor or blender, grind the walnuts, nutritional yeast, garlic powder, onion powder, turmeric, paprika, chipotle, mustard, and salt into a fine meal. Then add

1 tablespoon of the olive oil, the miso, water, and green chilis, and puree until combined. Season with salt and pepper to taste. Stuff each jalapeno half with the walnut filling, until the stuffing comes to the top edges of the pepper.

Time to set up your breading station. You'll need two plates and a bowl. Put ¼ cup of the flour on one plate, season with salt and pepper, and mix. Place your bowl next to that, add ½ cup of flour, and whisk in the milk until you have a smooth batter that's a bit thinner than that of pancakes. Season that with salt and pepper as well. On the remaining plate, season the bread crumbs with salt and pepper. Coat a baking sheet or casserole dish with the remaining 1 tablespoon of olive oil, and have it standing by for your breaded poppers.

Lightly coat each stuffed pepper with flour, then dip it into the wet batter, and then coat with the bread crumbs. The filling is thick enough that it won't fall out; just be gentle during the coating process to ensure it stays put. Place the stuffed and breaded peppers on your cooking vessel, give them a light spritz of oil or cooking spray, and bake until golden brown, 30 to 35 minutes. Let cool for 5 minutes unless you love blisters on the roof of your mouth.

TIP

Be sure to wash your hands thoroughly after handling any hot peppers, or else you'll be in a world of hurt the next time you touch your eyes, or your wang, or your vajayjay. I always keep a box of latex gloves on hand for hot-pepper handling.

JUANITO'S SALSA

|||||||||||||||||||||||||||||||||||||||||||||||||||||||||||||||||||||||||||||||||||||||||||||||||||||||||||

Juanito is a guy I once worked with. He made this salsa. It was awesome.

Makes 3 cups

4 Roma tomatoes
1 or 2 jalapeno peppers (depending on how spicy you like it;
    see Tip, page 185)
½ red bell pepper, seeded
½ yellow onion, cut into rounds
2 tablespoons chopped fresh cilantro
1 clove garlic
¼ teaspoon cumin
Salt and pepper
1 medium avocado, roughly chopped
½ teaspoon fresh lime juice

Heat a lightly oiled grill or grill pan over medium-high heat. Place the tomatoes, jalapeno, bell pepper, and onion on the grill or grill pan. Grill, turning occasionally, until they become tender and the outsides are slightly charred (8 to 10 minutes for the jalapeno, bell pepper, and onion; 15 to 18 minutes for the tomatoes). Let cool. Chop the veggies into manageable pieces. In a blender or food processor, puree the veggies with the cilantro, garlic, cumin, and a pinch of salt and a pinch of pepper. Add the avocado and lime juice, and puree until smooth. Season with salt and pepper to taste. Store in a sealed container in the fridge for up to a week.

PICO DE GALLO

|||||||||||||||||||||||||||||||||||||||||||||||||||||||||||||||||||||||||||||||||||||||||||||||||||||||||||

Everybody should know how to make pico de gallo. And now you will. Make it ahead of time to allow the flavors to develop for a few hours or even overnight.

Makes 2 cups

1½ pounds Roma tomatoes, diced
¾ cup diced red onion
½ jalapeno pepper, seeded and minced, (see Tip, page 185)
1 tablespoon fresh lime juice
2 tablespoons chopped fresh cilantro
2 tablespoons extra-virgin olive oil
Salt and pepper

Mix the tomatoes, onion, jalapeno, lime juice, cilantro, and oil. Season with salt and pepper to taste. Store in a sealed container in the fridge for up to a week.

LA CARGA DE LA MADRE

This multilayered bean dip is like the end of a *Seinfeld* episode, when all the things that happened earlier converge, usually resulting in some sort of misfortune. But instead of these things coming around to bite you in the ass, you get to do the biting. Grab a bag of tortilla chips and behold! La Carga de la Madre!!

Serves 12 as an appetizer

4 cups Homemade Refried Beans (see recipe, page 189), or
    use organic canned vegan beans
1½ cups Not Yo Mama's Cheeze Sauce (see recipe, page 216)
    or 8 ounces shredded vegan cheddar cheeze
1½ cups Sour Creaminess (see recipe, page 205) or other
    vegan sour cream)
2 cups Gargantuan Guac (see recipe, page 183)
2 cups shredded green cabbage
2 cups Pico de Gallo (see recipe, page 187)
¼ cup thinly sliced scallions

In a medium pot, heat the beans on medium-low until warmed through. Spread the beans evenly in a 12-inch casserole dish or pie pan. Evenly spread the cheeze sauce over the beans. Spread a layer of sour creaminess over the cheeze sauce, then spread a layer of guacamole over the sour creaminess. Top the guacamole with the cabbage, then top the cabbage with the pico de gallo. Finally, sprinkle the scallions on top, and serve immediately.

HOMEMADE REFRIED BEANS

||||||||||||||||||||||||||||||||||||||||||||||||||||||||||||||||||||||||||||||||||||||||||||||||||||||||||||||||||||||

Makes 4 cups

1 pound dry pinto beans
1 bay leaf
1 cup extra-virgin olive oil
1 cup thinly sliced scallions
6 cloves garlic
1 dried arbol chili
Salt and pepper

Soak the beans in water, in the fridge, for at least 8 hours. They will almost double in size, so make sure the water covers them by at least 3 inches. After soaking, drain and rinse the beans thoroughly. Put them in a large pot, and add water until it covers the beans by about 1½ inches. Add the bay leaf, bring to a boil, then reduce heat and simmer for about 1 hour. When the beans are soft, they're ready.

In the meantime, in a small saucepan, heat the olive oil, scallions, garlic cloves, and arbol chili over medium heat until the oil starts to boil. Let simmer for 6 to 8 minutes, or until the garlic is soft and golden brown, then turn the heat off, and let the oil cool to room temperature. Remove the dried chili.

Now that your beans are fully cooked, remove the bay leaf, and mash them right in the pot with a potato masher to the consistency you like. Note that while they are hot, the mashed beans will have a soupy texture, but as they cool, they will thicken.

Finally, add the scallions and garlic to the mashed beans and stir. Also add as much or as little of the oil as you please, depending on how much fat you want. Season with salt and pepper to taste, mash it all together one last time, and your refried beans are ready.

CHAPTER 10
condiments
and sauces

|||||||||||||||||||||||||||||||||||||||||||||||||||||||||||||||||||||||||||||||||||||||||||||||||||||||||||||||||

EVERYBODY LIKES TO HAVE STUFF TO PUT ON OTHER STUFF. I personally enjoy putting stuff on top of the stuff that I put on the first stuff, but that's just me. All the stuff in this chapter fits into the "stuff to put on other stuff" category. Not only are the following items used in other recipes throughout the book; they are specially designed to have protective powers. For instance, not only is the Crazy Shit (see page 194) good on just about every single food item you could possibly imagine, but a small amount smeared on your doorstep wards off both hobgoblins and regular goblins.

THE CRAZY SHIT AND
THE CRAZY SHIT VINEGAR

||||||||||||||||||||||||||||||||||||||||||||||||||||||||||||||||||||||||||||||||||||||||||||||||||||||||||||||||||||||||||||||||||||||

This tasty relish goes on anything and everything. Add it to sandwiches, tacos, burritos, burgers, veggie dogs, salads, dressings, and dips. The vinegar can be used when you want to add a punch of flavor, a kick of heat, and a flying elbow drop of awesomeness to dressings and sauces. I keep both of these items on hand at all times. The relish will keep for about three weeks in a sealed container in the fridge, and the vinegar will keep for 2 to 3 months in a mason jar in the fridge.

Makes about 1 cup of Crazy Shit and about 1½ cups of Crazy Shit Vinegar

2 cups distilled white vinegar
4 tablespoons unrefined granulated sugar
½ medium red bell pepper, sliced into ¼-inch-thick strips
2 medium carrots, cut into ¼-inch-thick slices
1 jalapeno pepper, cut into ¼-inch-thick slices
½ medium yellow onion, thinly sliced

In a saucepan, bring the vinegar and sugar to a boil. Reduce to a simmer, and stir until the sugar is completely dissolved. Add the bell pepper, carrots, jalapeno, and onion, and simmer for 1 more minute, then turn off the heat. Transfer to a bowl, and set aside to cool to room temperature. And don't be all hasty and put it in the fridge to cool it faster — it needs this time to develop the flavors.

When it's cool, drain liquid from the vegetables, but *do not throw away the liquid!!!* That vinegar is now infused with all those great flavors, and it will last for months in a sealed container in the fridge. It will be used elsewhere in this book under the name *crazy shit vinegar* (I'm so creative).

In a blender or food processor, pulse about half of the veggies until they are chopped into a relish-like form. Transfer them to a bowl, and repeat with the rest of the veggies. We don't want them pureed, just chopped really finely. That's why we do it in two batches. And they don't need no salt, pepper, oil — nothing!!

TIP

Make extra Crazy Shit and instead of processing it, keep the veggies whole as a great accoutrement to tacos or a garnish for the Dirty Dudetini (see recipe, page 14).

BARBECRAZYSHIT SAUCE

|||||||||||||||||||||||||||||||||||||||||||||||||||||||||||||||||||||||||||||||||||||||||||||||||

Use this for all your barbecue needs. It's sweet *and* smoky...like when a piece of candy has sex with some smoke, and they have a kid. You'll see what I mean when you make it.

Makes 4 cups

2 teaspoons extra-virgin olive oil
1 cup diced yellow onion
Salt
3 cloves garlic, chopped
¼ cup fresh orange juice
⅔ cup Crazy Shit Vinegar (see recipe, page 194) or apple cider vinegar
2 cups ketchup
¼ cup water
1 tablespoon molasses
2 tablespoons yellow mustard
1 drop liquid smoke (see WTF, page 32)
Pepper

In a saucepan, heat the oil over medium heat, and add the onion with a pinch of salt. Cook for 4 to 5 minutes, until the onion is soft. Add the garlic, and cook for 3 to 4 more minutes. Add the orange juice and vinegar, and cook for 3 to 4 more minutes, until reduced by half. Then whisk in the ketchup, water, molasses, mustard, and liquid smoke, and gently simmer for about 15 minutes. Season with salt and pepper to taste.

KAJILLION ISLAND DRESSING

It's like Thousand Island dressing, with a lot more zeros.

Makes 1 cup

½ cup vegan mayo (see WTF, page 42)
¼ cup Crazy Shit (see recipe, page 194)
¼ cup ketchup
2 tablespoons yellow mustard

Put it all in a bowl and whisk it together. Boom!

DREAMY TAHINI DRESSING

Keep it as is for slathering on sandwiches and burgers, or thin it out with a little water for a creamy salad dressing.

Makes 1½ cups

½ cup tahini
2 tablespoons fresh lemon juice
½ cup water
½ clove garlic
2 teaspoons chopped fresh Italian parsley
2 teaspoons chopped fresh mint
1 teaspoon extra-virgin olive oil
Pinch of smoked paprika
Salt and pepper

In a food processor or blender, combine the tahini, lemon juice, water, garlic, parsley, mint, oil, and paprika, and puree until smooth. Season to taste with salt and pepper.

BALSAMIC GLAZE

I have an aunt who, for the life of her, cannot say the word *balsamic*. It always comes out as *boz-monic*. She also says *tur-let* instead of *toilet*. And since I have made fun of her for it for years, I now catch myself saying it. So please enjoy this boz-moni— (get out of my head, Aunt Donna!!) I mean *balsamic* — glaze drizzled on pizzas, salads, desserts, and fruit.

Makes ⅔ cup

2 cups balsamic vinegar
¼ cup brown sugar
Salt and pepper

In a small pot, bring the vinegar and sugar to a boil. Reduce the heat to low, and stir until the sugar is completely dissolved. Simmer for 10 to 15 minutes, until it reduces by two-thirds and thickens. Season to taste with salt and pepper.

THE TOMATO KILLER

||||||||||||||||||||||||||||||||||||||||||||||||||||||||||||||||||||||||||||||||||||||||||||||||||||

This is my go-to tomato sauce. Pasta, pizza, cereal — it goes on everything. I don't kill flies or spiders, but I'll murder the crap out of some tomatoes.

Makes 2 cups

2 pounds Roma tomatoes
4 teaspoons extra-virgin olive oil
Salt and pepper
6 cloves garlic, sliced
1 tablespoon chopped fresh oregano
Pinch of chili flakes
1 tablespoon chopped oil-packed sun-dried tomatoes
2 tablespoons roughly chopped fresh basil leaves

Preheat the oven to 400°F. Toss the whole tomatoes with 2 teaspoons of the oil and a healthy pinch of salt and a pinch of pepper. In the roasting vessel of your choice, lay out the tomatoes so they're not all up in each other's shit (leaving a little space between them allows for more even browning), and roast them in the oven for about 1 hour, turning them over after 30 minutes. When they're soft and browned, they're done. Remove, and let cool.

In a saucepan, heat the remaining 2 teaspoons of oil over medium heat, and add the garlic, oregano, and chili flakes. Cook for 2 to 3 minutes, or until the garlic begins to brown around the edges. Add the sun-dried tomatoes, the roasted tomatoes, and a pinch of salt. With a wooden spoon, break apart the tomatoes so their juice comes out, and simmer for 5 minutes.

Carefully pour the contents of the pan into a food processor or blender, add the fresh basil, and puree. Return the pureed sauce to the pan, bring to a simmer, and cook for 5 more minutes. Season with salt and pepper to taste, and it's done!

VARIATION

Instead of using fresh tomatoes and roasting them yourself, you can be lazy and use one 28-ounce can of fire-roasted diced tomatoes.

FAUXLOGNESE SAUCE

|||||||||||||||||||||||||||||||||||||||||||||||||||||||||||||||||||||||||||||||||||||||||||||||||||||||||||||||||

Thick and "meaty," without all the grease.

Makes 4 cups

One 14-ounce block extra-firm tofu, drained (see Tip, page 35)
1 teaspoon dried oregano
1 teaspoon dried basil
½ teaspoon dried thyme
½ teaspoon fennel seeds
¼ teaspoon chili flakes
½ teaspoon garlic powder
½ teaspoon onion powder
1 tablespoon nutritional yeast (see WTF, page 27)
¼ teaspoon salt, plus more as needed
1 tablespoon extra-virgin olive oil, plus more to lube the baking dish
1 teaspoon vegan Worcestershire sauce (see WTF, page 12)
2 cups Tomato Killer (see recipe, page 200) or other tomato sauce
Pepper

Preheat the oven to 400°F. In a large bowl, combine the tofu, oregano, basil, thyme, fennel, chili flakes, garlic powder, onion powder, nutritional yeast, salt, the 1 tablespoon of oil, and the Worcestershire. With a fork, potato masher, or your very clean hands, mash everything together until the tofu is completely "ground" and coated with spices. Lube up a casserole or baking dish with olive oil, and spread out the tofu mixture in it evenly. To ensure that it browns properly, make sure the layer is no more than ½ inch thick, using a second dish if necessary.

Bake the mixture for 30 minutes, then remove it from the oven. The top of the mixture should be lightly browned at this point. Toss it around with a spatula to allow the other side to brown. Return the mixture to the oven and cook for 30 more minutes, or until the mixture is mostly browned with some moist, white tofu-looking parts remaining.

In a large saucepan, stir together the tomato sauce and the tofu mixture, and cook over medium heat. When it gets to a simmer, it's done. Season with salt and pepper to taste.

PEANUT SAUCE

Great as a dipping sauce or for tossing with noodles.

Makes 1½ cups

½ cup coconut milk
½ cup smooth peanut butter
2 teaspoons low-sodium tamari or soy sauce (see WTF, page 25)
½ teaspoon Sriracha or Thai chili sauce
2 teaspoons fresh lime juice
¼ cup water
Salt and pepper

Whisk together the coconut milk, peanut butter, tamari, Sriracha or chili sauce, lime juice, and water until smooth. Season with salt and pepper to taste.

SOUR CREAMINESS

||||||||||||||||||||||||||||||||||||||||||||||||||||||||||||||||||||||||||||||||||||||||||||||||||||||||||||

There are a couple of great vegan store-bought sour creams out there. You can get them at a health food store or on the interwebs — but it's not too difficult to make a comparable sour cream at home. Here's mine.

Makes ¾ cup

One 12-ounce package firm silken tofu (the one in the
cardboard box)
2 tablespoons fresh lemon juice
1 tablespoon Crazy Shit Vinegar (see recipe, page 194)
1 teaspoon agave nectar
¾ teaspoon salt

In a food processor or blender, blend all ingredients for several minutes, until creamy and smooth.

CHILI TOPPING

||||||||||||||||||||||||||||||||||||||||||||||||||||||||||||||||||||||||||||||||||||||||||||||||||||||||||||||

I'm not really sure what came first, my love for chili as a food topping, or my love for Chili of '90s R&B sensation TLC. Either way I think they are both equally delicious. One of them I'd place on top of a burger, and one of them I'd place on top of…um…well, let's just stick with the food angle for right now.

Makes 2 cups

One 8-ounce package tempeh
1 teaspoon extra-virgin olive oil
⅔ cup diced yellow onion
Pinch of salt, plus more as needed
3 cloves garlic, chopped
4 tablespoons chili powder
Pinch of cayenne pepper
2 teaspoons ground cumin
1 teaspoon dried oregano
2 tablespoons tomato paste
2 cups water
½ teaspoon molasses
Pepper

Using a steamer basket, steam the tempeh for 25 to 30 minutes, and let cool. Then break it up with your very clean hands until it's completely crumbled…like my faith in George Lucas and all he does.

In a medium skillet, heat the oil over medium-high heat, and add the onion and a pinch of salt. Saute for 4 to 5 minutes, until the onion becomes soft and lightly browned. Reduce the heat to medium, add the garlic, tempeh, chili powder, cayenne, cumin, and oregano, and cook for 2 to 3 more minutes.

Stir in the tomato paste, add the water, and bring to a simmer.

When the mixture thickens (after 3 to 5 minutes of simmering), add the molasses, and let simmer for 5 more minutes. Season with salt and pepper to taste.

HTF did I come up with this recipe?

Once my friends and I got our driver's licenses, we began to take our first unsupervised outings to Waltz's, the local ice cream shop/golf ball driving range/hot dog stand. We had grown up going there, but until then we had always needed the presence of an adult for both transportation and ice cream procurement purposes. We would each scarf down two or three of their town-famous chili dogs and a vanilla soft-serve cone with that strawberry dip stuff that would get hard... classic. But now, armed with licenses to drive and some money of our own, we were let loose on the town.

It's interesting what one chooses to do when newly unsupervised. It's like when your puppy accidentally gets off the leash: she unwittingly runs twenty feet away from you and realizes she can now do anything she wants, but she's so overwhelmed with excitement that she doesn't know what to do first. Our first order of business was to get a basket of golf balls at Waltz's driving range and try to hit them onto the highway. Perfectly reasonable, right? The way Waltz's driving range was situated, this was not an easy task, but it was possible, which made it nice and competitive.

This activity was actually a bit of a step up from our usual throwing of apples at the big rigs from the overpass, and it didn't leave as much evidence. (When my mom and I drove over that bridge the next day, she would say something like, "What's with these apples on the road all the time?" And I'd be like, "Hmm. I dunno. That's weird.")

We, of course, didn't realize how incredibly dangerous these activities were, and fortunately nothing really bad ever happened. We eventually stopped throwing stuff at cars and became interested in seeing girls' boobs, which was a clear sign of growth. But I still get a little misty-eyed when I see someone hitting an apple with a golf club (*sob*).

In memory of old man Waltz (I'm pretty sure he's dead, but I'm not positive), I created this chili topping to go on nachos, burgers, and, of course, veggie dogs with minced yellow onion.

SEITAN SEASONING

|||||||||||||||||||||||||||||||||||||||||||||||||||||||||||||||||||||||||||||||||||||||||||||||||||||||||||||||||||

I make at least a triple batch of this, so I always have it on hand. It's a huge time-saver when you want to whip up some seitan. I guess I could have just done the multiplication for you here and presented a triple batch, but I didn't.

Makes approximately 3 tablespoons

2 tablespoons nutritional yeast (see WTF, page 27)
1 teaspoon garlic powder
1 teaspoon onion powder
1 teaspoon vegetable bouillon powder
½ teaspoon pepper
½ teaspoon celery seed
¼ teaspoon dried thyme
¼ teaspoon ground sage

Whisk all ingredients together, and store in an airtight container.

SCRAMBLE SEASONING

I'll tell you the same thing here as I did for the seitan seasoning: make a triple batch…and no, I didn't do the math for you here either. Also, you'll see black salt as an ingredient below. It's perfect for a scramble because it has a high sulfur content, which makes it smell kind of like eggs…if they farted. Find it at an Indian market or on the interwebs. Very cool stuff.

Makes approximately 2½ tablespoons

1 tablespoon nutritional yeast (see WTF, page 27)
1 teaspoon chili powder
1 teaspoon black salt
½ teaspoon cumin
½ teaspoon dried oregano
¼ teaspoon turmeric
¼ teaspoon pepper

Whisk all ingredients together, and store in an airtight container.

BLACKENED SEASONING

Use this rub when grilling seitan, tofu, tempeh, or veggies. As with my other seasonings, make extra.

Makes approximately 5 tablespoons

1½ tablespoons paprika
1 tablespoon garlic powder
1 tablespoon onion powder
1 teaspoon cayenne pepper
1 teaspoon dried basil
1 teaspoon dried oregano
1 teaspoon unrefined granulated sugar
½ teaspoon salt
1 teaspoon pepper

Whisk all ingredients together, and store in an airtight container.

PARMESAN TOPPING

||||||||||||||||||||||||||||||||||||||||||||||||||||||||||||||||||||||||||||||||||||||||||||||||||||||||||||||

Use this on pastas, salads, and pizzas, and if you want your dog to look at you funny, sprinkle a little on her head.

Makes 1 cup

½ cup coarsely chopped raw walnuts
½ cup nutritional yeast (see WTF, page 27)
Salt

Preheat the oven to 350°F, spread out the walnuts on a baking sheet, and toast them in the oven for 5 minutes. Take them out and let cool.

In a food processor or blender, grind the toasted walnuts into a meal. Scrape down the sides of the container if necessary, and then add the nutritional yeast and a pinch of salt. Pulse a few more times until the ingredients are combined. Store in an airtight container.

HOLLANDAZE SAUCE

||||||||||||||||||||||||||||||||||||||||||||||||||||||||||||||||||||||||||||||||||||||||||||||||||||||||||

While this *sounds* like a menu item you might find in a cafe in Amsterdam, it is nothing more than a creamy sauce that's perfect on broccoli, asparagus, or a Morning Benediction (see recipe, page 48).

Makes 1⅓ cups

One 12-ounce package soft silken tofu
2 tablespoons nutritional yeast (see WTF, page 27)
1 tablespoon fresh lemon juice
¼ teaspoon mustard powder
¼ teaspoon turmeric
¼ teaspoon black salt
¼ teaspoon paprika
2 tablespoons vegan margarine, melted
Sea salt and pepper

In a food processor or blender, combine the tofu, nutritional yeast, lemon juice, mustard powder, turmeric, black salt, paprika, and margarine, and process until smooth. Season with sea salt and pepper to taste.

CASHEW RICOTTA

||||||||||||||||||||||||||||||||||||||||||||||||||||||||||||||||||||||||||||||||||||||||||||||||||||||||||||||||||||||

Stuff this into anything that ends in the letter *i*.

Makes 3 cups

2 cups whole raw cashews
One 14-ounce can artichoke hearts, drained, rinsed, and
    roughly chopped
2 tablespoons fresh lemon juice
1 cup water
1½ teaspoons salt, plus more as needed
1 clove garlic
1 heaping tablespoon nutritional yeast (see WTF, page 27)
2 teaspoons extra-virgin olive oil
Pepper

In a medium pot, cover the cashews with water, and boil for 8 minutes to soften them up. Drain and let cool. In a food processor or blender, process the cashews until they're finely ground. Add the artichokes, lemon juice, water, salt, garlic, nutritional yeast, and oil, and puree until smooth. Season with salt and pepper to taste.

NOT-ZZARELLA SAUCE

Put this on pizza or a fake-meatball hoagie. (I'm thinking that *hoagie* is the fattest word in our lexicon. *H-O-A-G-I-E*. It just sounds fat in every way.)

Makes 3½ cups

1 cup whole raw cashews
One 12-ounce package soft silken tofu
¼ teaspoon mustard powder
¼ teaspoon garlic powder
¼ teaspoon onion powder
½ teaspoon yellow miso
½ teaspoon salt
2 teaspoons extra-virgin olive oil
1 teaspoon dried basil
2 tablespoons nutritional yeast (see WTF, page 27)
⅔ cup water

In a small pot, cover the cashews with water, and boil for about 8 minutes to soften them up. Drain and let cool. In a food processor or blender, process the cashews until they're finely ground. Add the tofu, mustard powder, garlic powder, onion powder, miso, salt, oil, basil, nutritional yeast, and water. Puree till the sauce is as smooth as Kenny G's sax licks…and that's pretty goddamned smooth.

SMOKED CHEDDAR SAUCE

||||||||||||||||||||||||||||||||||||||||||||||||||||||||||||||||||||||||||||||||||||||||||||||||||||||||||||||||

Top some french fries with the chili topping (see page 206) and drizzle this over it. Oh damn! I just did that thing when saliva involuntarily squirts from the back of your mouth and goes like 2 feet. I knew a guy in college who could do that at will. He was cool.

Makes 3½ cups

1 cup whole raw cashews
One 12-ounce package soft silken tofu
¼ teaspoon garlic powder
¼ teaspoon onion powder
¼ teaspoon turmeric
¼ teaspoon liquid smoke (see WTF, page 32)
½ teaspoon yellow miso
½ teaspoon paprika
½ teaspoon salt
½ teaspoon mustard powder
2 teaspoons extra-virgin olive oil
2 tablespoons nutritional yeast (see WTF, page 27)
⅔ cup water

In a small pot, cover the cashews with water, and boil for about 8 minutes to soften them up. Drain and let cool. In a food processor or blender, process the cashews until they're finely ground. Add the tofu, garlic powder, onion powder, turmeric, liquid smoke, miso, paprika, salt, mustard powder, oil, nutritional yeast, and water. Puree till the sauce is as smooth as the following: "Excuse me, Miss, do you have a map? Because I keep getting lost in your eyes." Okay, well, maybe smoother than that.

NOT YO MAMA'S CHEEZE SAUCE

||||||||||||||||||||||||||||||||||||||||||||||||||||||||||||||||||||||||||||||||||||||||||||||||||||||||||||||||||||||||||

Say the first two words of the above title really fast...see what I did there? I rule.

Makes 3½ cups

1 cup whole raw cashews
One 12-ounce package soft silken tofu
¼ teaspoon garlic powder
¼ teaspoon onion powder
¼ teaspoon turmeric
½ teaspoon yellow miso
½ teaspoon paprika
½ teaspoon salt
Pinch of ground chipotle
2 teaspoons extra-virgin olive oil
2 tablespoons nutritional yeast (see WTF, page 27)
3 tablespoons water
2 tablespoons canned diced mild green chilis

In a small pot, cover the cashews with water, and boil for about 8 minutes to soften them up. Drain and let cool. In a food processor or blender, process the cashews until they're finely ground. Add the tofu, garlic powder, onion powder, turmeric, miso, paprika, salt, chipotle, oil, nutritional yeast, water, and chilis. Puree till the sauce is as smooth as Jean-Luc Picard's freshly shorn head.

BASIL PESTO

||||||||||||||||||||||||||||||||||||||||||||||||||||||||||||||||||||||||||||||||||||||||||||||

This versatile sauce should be a weapon in every cook's arsenal. It can be whipped up in no time, and added to pastas and pizzas, soups and sandwiches, and dips and dressings. Learn it. Love it. Eat it.

Makes 1½ cups

¼ cup raw pine nuts
1 packed cup fresh basil leaves
1 clove garlic, chopped
3 tablespoons Parmesan Topping (see recipe, page 211)
⅛ teaspoon salt, plus more as needed
Pepper
6 tablespoons extra-virgin olive oil

Heat a dry pan over medium-high heat, and cook the pine nuts for 1 to 2 minutes on one side, until they're slightly browned, then toss and cook for another 30 to 60 seconds (keep a close eye on them — they burn super easily). Let cool. In a food processor or blender, combine the pine nuts, basil, garlic, parmesan topping, salt, a pinch of pepper, and 2 tablespoons of the olive oil, and puree, scraping down the sides as needed. When it's all ground up, continue to blend, and pour in the remaining 4 tablespoons of olive oil in a steady stream. Season with salt and pepper to taste.

TIP
The Pesto Manifesto

Allow me to take this opportunity to proclaim that we are no longer shackled to basil-centric pesto sauces! We are free to incorporate an infinite assortment of ingredients in order to incite culinary inspiration! If you have a handful of nuts, some oil, garlic, and something green and leafy, you can make pesto. So use this basic pesto recipe as the key that opens the door to a world where cilantro pesto rains from the sky and arugula pesto tributaries feed spinach pesto waterfalls…and so on. With that, I give you…Basil Pesto!

BONUS CHAPTER
We All Scream!!
ice cream

|||||||||||||||||||||||||||||||||||||||||||||||||||||||||||||||||||||||||||||||||||||||||||||||||||||||||||||||

HERE ARE A FEW QUICK AND EASY ICE CREAM RECIPES sure to satisfy kids and stoners alike. You will need a food processor or blender and, of course, an ice cream maker. If you don't have both of these items, go do something else. But if you do have them, get ready to have the type of good old-fashioned family fun that would make Clark W. Griswold jealous.

NILLA

||||||||||||||||||||||||||||||||||||||||||||||||||||||||||||||||||||||||||||||||||||||||||||||||||||||||||

I've heard that there are vegan versions of those Nilla wafers we used to munch on as kids. I haven't found them yet (probably because I haven't really looked), but if you do, break them up into chunks and fold them into this recipe after it goes through the ice cream maker.

Serves 4

One 12-ounce package soft silken tofu
⅓ cup agave nectar
¼ cup coconut milk
Seeds from 1 vanilla bean
Pinch of salt

In a food processor or blender, combine all ingredients. Puree until smooth, then put your ice cream maker to work.

RASPBERRY HIBISCUS

||||||||||||||||||||||||||||||||||||||||||||||||||||||||||||||||||||||||||||||||||||||||||||||||||||||||||

This is a fantastic summer dessert. If only there was a frozen alcoholic beverage with similar flavorings to accompany such a dessert. Hmm...

Serves 4

One 12-ounce package soft silken tofu
½ cup fresh or frozen raspberries
⅓ cup hibiscus syrup (see recipe, page 17)
¼ cup coconut milk
Pinch of salt

In a food processor or blender, combine all ingredients. Puree until smooth, then put your ice cream maker to work.

THE GREEN GOBLIN

|||||||||||||||||||||||||||||||||||||||||||||||||||||||||||||||||||||||||||||||||||||||||||||||||

Pistachios are *the* best nuts. Avocados are *the* best of whatever they are. I think they're fruit? Yes, fruit. So I thought, "Why not team them up?" Turned out pretty darn good. And while the end product *is* green, there's nothing really goblin-y about it. I just liked the alliteration.

Serves 4

2 ounces dark chocolate or dark chocolate chips
½ cup roasted unsalted shelled pistachios
One 12-ounce package soft silken tofu
⅓ cup plus 1 tablespoon agave nectar
1½ teaspoons fresh lime juice
¼ cup coconut milk
1 medium Hass avocado, pitted and removed from skin
Pinch of salt

Line a dish or baking sheet with parchment paper. In a medium glass or metal bowl set on top of a pot of simmering water, melt the chocolate, stirring occasionally. Stir in the pistachios. Once they are coated, remove with a fork and place them on the parchment paper, making sure they are separated so they don't stick together. Place the pistachios in the fridge for 20 minutes, or until the chocolate hardens.

In a food processor or blender, combine the tofu, agave, lime juice, coconut milk, avocado, and salt, and puree until smooth. Then put your ice cream maker to work. Finally, stir the chocolate-covered pistachios into the prepared ice cream.

THE SAILOR'S
PEANUT BUTTER RUM

||||||||||||||||||||||||||||||||||||||||||||||||||||||||||||||||||||||||||||||||||||||||||||||||||||||||

Shiver me timbers! It's ice cream that tastes like rum! And peanut butter! Sit me down in front of a *Law & Order* marathon, and I'm good to go. Nothing past the Briscoe years, obviously.

Serves 4

One 12-ounce package soft silken tofu
¼ cup coconut milk
3 tablespoons smooth peanut butter
⅓ cup Sailor Syrup (see recipe, page 55), plus 1 tablespoon
    for garnish
1 teaspoon vanilla extract
Pinch of salt
1 tablespoon chopped peanuts, for garnish

In a food processor or blender, combine the tofu, coconut milk, peanut butter, the ⅓ cup of syrup, the vanilla, and salt, and puree until smooth. Then put your ice cream maker to work. Serve it topped with chopped peanuts and a drizzle of sailor syrup.

URLs ||||||||||||||||||||||||||||||||||||||||||||||||||||||||||||||||||||||||||||||||||||||||
for Accompanying Videos

In case for some reason you don't possess the ability to scan the QR codes in this book — like maybe you only have a dumbphone instead of a smartphone, or you prefer to use one of those old-fashioned computer thingys to surf the interwebs instead of using a tablet — I have been gracious enough to supply the URLs for each of the videos that accompany this book. What a "man of the people" I am!

Page 7 and back cover: http://www.thesexyvegan.com/trailer

Page 25, Seitan Slices: http://youtu.be/XFk-8kDnGwA

Page 25, Seitan Cutlets: http://youtu.be/ftugwvHQ6ug

Page 29, Pretend Italian Sausages: http://youtu.be/aukyfydaUfg

Page 33, Tempeh Bacon: http://youtu.be/WgT_tKxe9Ok

Page 48, Morning Benediction: http://youtu.be/yL9vASucOuU

Page 86, The Beet Down: http://youtu.be/VglXcUQR6hw

Page 107, The Portly Fellow: http://youtu.be/5khX9zv_fPo

Page 136, Barbecue Ribz: http://youtu.be/4BiM9VujjBY

Page 143, Grilled "Fish" Tacos: http://youtu.be/IIxlZzvjn1M

Page 147, Celery Root Oven Fries: http://youtu.be/rPRh3LPAis8

Page 179, Golden Beet Hummus (variation):
    http://youtu.be/44BQjg0H8RE

Page 179, Golden Beet Hummus (roasting beets):
    http://youtu.be/VglXcUQR6hw

Page 180, Buffalo Wangs: http://youtu.be/HD7cAm9ucEA

Page 183, Gargantuan Guac: http://youtu.be/OjFMbKsP1ns

Index ||||||||||||||||||||||||||||||||||||||||||||||||||||||||||||||||||||||||||||||||||||||||||||||||||||||||||||||||||||||||||||||||||||||||||||||||||||||▶

For entries in which there is more than one page reference, references in **red print** indicate the original recipe; references in normal print indicate recipes in which it is used as an ingredient.

About the Author ||||||||||||||||||||||||||||||||||||||||||||||||||||||||||||

BRIAN L. PATTON is the executive chef for Vegin' Out, a vegan food delivery service in Los Angeles. The quintessential "regular dude" vegan chef, he started posting instructional cooking videos on YouTube as his witty, ukulele-playing alter ego "The Sexy Vegan" and quickly gained a large following. Brian offers his popular cooking demonstrations at stores, restaurants, and community centers throughout Southern California and in his travels around the country.

www.thesexyvegan.com

NEW WORLD LIBRARY is dedicated to publishing books and other media that inspire and challenge us to improve the quality of our lives and the world.

We are a socially and environmentally aware company, and we strive to embody the ideals presented in our publications. We recognize that we have an ethical responsibility to our customers, our staff members, and our planet.

We serve our customers by creating the finest publications possible on personal growth, creativity, spirituality, wellness, and other areas of emerging importance. We serve New World Library employees with generous benefits, significant profit sharing, and constant encouragement to pursue their most expansive dreams.

As a member of the Green Press Initiative, we print an increasing number of books with soy-based ink on 100 percent postconsumer-waste recycled paper. Also, we power our offices with solar energy and contribute to nonprofit organizations working to make the world a better place for us all.

Our products are available
in bookstores everywhere.
For our catalog, please contact:

New World Library
14 Pamaron Way
Novato, California 94949

Phone: 415-884-2100 or 800-972-6657
Catalog requests: Ext. 50
Orders: Ext. 52
Fax: 415-884-2199
Email: escort@newworldlibrary.com

To subscribe to our electronic newsletter, visit
www.newworldlibrary.com